The aim of the Biblical Classics Library is to make
available at the lowest prices new editions of
classic titles by well-known scholars. There is
a particular emphasis on making these books
affordable to Eastern Europe and the
Two-Thirds World.

For current listing see overleaf

Introducing Old Testament Theology

D1386684

Authors in the Biblical Classics Library:

C.K. Barrett
  The Signs of an Apostle (19)
F.F. Bruce
  Men and Movements in the Primitive Church (13)
  The Message of the New Testament (1)
  The Pauline Circle (14)
David Burnett
  The Healing of the Nations (18)
D.A. Carson
  From Triumphalism to Maturity (20)
  Jesus and His Friends (15)
  The Sermon on the Mount (2)
  When Jesus Confronts the World (16)
H.L. Ellison
  Men Spake from God (9)
  The Message of the Old Testament (3)
John Goldingay
  God's Prophet, God's Servant (5)
Graeme Goldsworthy
  Gospel and Kingdom (4)
  Gospel and Wisdom (10)
  The Gospel in Revelation (6)
J.H. Greenlee
  Scribes, Scrolls and Scripture (17)
A.M. Hunter
  Introducing New Testament Theology (26)
R.T. Kendall
  Believing God (11)
  Does Jesus Care? (25)
  Jonah (12)
  Once Saved, Always Saved (28)
I. Howard Marshall
  The Work of Christ (7)
Leon Morris
  The Cross of Jesus (8)
J.N. Schofield
  Introducing Old Testament Theology (27)
Thomas Smail
  The Forgotten Father (23)
Helmut Thielicke
  A Little Exercise for Young Theologians (24)
John Wenham
  Easter Enigma (22)
A.M. Wolters
  Creation Regained (21)

Introducing Old Testament Theology

J.N. Schofield

paternoster
press

Copyright © 1964 SCM Press Ltd.

First published in the UK 1964
by SCM Press Ltd, 9–17 St Albans Place, London

This edition published 1997 by
Paternoster Press in the Biblical Classics Library

03 02 01 00 99 98 97   7 6 5 4 3 2 1

Paternoster Press in an imprint of Paternoster Publishing,
P.O. Box 300, Carlisle, Cumbria CA3 0QS

British Library Cataloguing in Publication Data

A catalogue record for this book is available from the British Library.

ISBN 0–85364–778–x

Printed in Great Britain by Mackays of Chatham PLC, Kent

CONTENTS

CONTENTS

PREFACE

IN THE past five years some large books on Old Testament theology have appeared in English, and when I was asked to write a shorter book to introduce the subject I welcomed the suggestion in the hope that readers may become interested and make use of the fuller presentations. The subject is important because the existence and nature of God is the ultimate concern of thinking people, and the knowledge of God presented by the Old Testament is basic to the faith of Jews, Christians and Mohammedans. The fact of evil and the possibility of progress are constantly recurring themes in modern thought. They are central to Old Testament theology, where both are shown in the light of the tireless movement of a gracious purpose.

To understand the Old Testament we must use the results of archaeological and historical research, the comparative study of religious, and literary and linguistic studies to enable us to reconstruct the course of the actual history, the growth of the literature and the development of the religion. But the theology must be the theology of the book in its final form. Ancient history and tradition, primitive ideas from outside religions, the records of experiences of men who believed they had seen God in action and heard him speak—all were fused in the crucible of the situation and experience of the latest editors. The unity is a living process in which the one God is always active in historical events, and speaking through individuals who interpreted them. Through many centuries countless men and women have heard through the pages of the Old Testament the 'word' of the same God, and the book has an intrinsic validity as divine revelation as well as a relationship to its sequel in the New Testament.

I wish to express my gratitude to those who have read the book in typescript and so willingly and freely given me help and advice: Professors D. Winton Thomas and N. W. Porteous, Doctors A. R. Vidler and O. Wyon, and the Rev. D. L. Edwards.

Except in a few places where I have given my own translation of the Hebrew text, the quotations are from the American Revised Standard Version.

J. N. SCHOFIELD

INTRODUCTION

Approaching the Old Testament

THE WHOLE Bible is propaganda, written for a purpose, and humanly speaking it is because it is propaganda that it has survived. The author of John (20.30 f.; 21.25) wrote 'Now Jesus did many other signs in the presence of the disciples, which are not written in this book; but these are written that you may believe that Jesus is the Christ, the Son of God, and that believing you may have life in his name.' The New Testament was written and preserved because an ever-increasing number of men and women, scattered throughout the Roman Empire, believed that Jesus of Nazareth was the Messiah foretold in the Old Testament, and the one who had brought salvation to the world. They themselves had found peace with the God he called Father, victory in their struggles, and a new and joyful way of living their daily life. Stories and sayings of Jesus were remembered by those who had lived with him. They were used in teaching, preaching and worship. Some of them were written down and circulated; and from this mass of material, oral and written, each evangelist made his selection to prove a special truth or serve a definite purpose.

Similarly the Old Testament stories were retained and rewritten because a small group of Jews, descendants of those who had been taken captive to Babylonia, believed themselves to be the sole survivors of the Hebrew people whose glorious traditions ran back into the dim past. They re-used the old stories, adapted them in up-to-date preaching to the needs of their own age, and enriched them with their own experiences of contact with the same God who had moulded the lives of their forefathers. There is a human reason why each story and saying was written and retained when so much was discarded and lost, and it is much more important in biblical study to try to discover why a story was told or a saying recorded than to question its date, origin or historicity. The Old Testament writers and editors believed themselves to be part of the people whom God had chosen and called to be the medium through which he could reveal himself, and they so shaped and arranged ancient myths, national legends, traditions and history as to make them a record wherein men could find and meet God, and hear him speaking the revealing word. The reasons for writing and preserving, when we can find them, help us to understand the meaning the writers and compilers intended to convey; they reflect the message and purpose of the Bible. When we listen to New Testament parables our first question is 'Why was it told? what is its meaning and message?' and not 'Did it actually happen?' The details are often unimportant, and if we discovered that the story had an earlier form before it was used by Jesus the main value of the discovery would be that by comparing the two forms we could see how, in altering the original story, Jesus had made his reason for telling it, and his message through it, more clear. So with the Old Testament our first question must be, why was the story or saying told, what purpose has the writer in shaping the tradition or history in this way?

There is another equally important question. What is the *provenance* of the story?—where, by whom, and for whom was it written or told? The place and the circle of thought or outlook from which the story came are as important as the date. Are the differences between the four Gospels accounted for by the fact that they were written one after the other, or that they were written in different places and so sprang from different *milieux* of outlook rather than of time? The history of Israel was told in one way in the books from Genesis to Kings and in another in the Chronicles. Both begin with Adam and Eve and carry the account on beyond the Babylonian exile; do they differ because of the date at which they were written or because they spring from different circles of thought? Perhaps in both

Testaments the stories were preserved in different ways to meet the needs of different people in different places rather than at different times. In *The Rebirth of Christianity* S. A. Cook suggested that the Old Testament is not the outcome of 'progressive revelation' in a time sequence, but of the action and reaction between different groups of people living at the same time although in different circles of thought or practice, such as might be represented today by Anglicans, Baptists, Methodists, Presbyterians, Quakers, and Roman Catholics. If we were given six cuttings from journals, each representing one of these points of view, and were asked to put them in their chronological order, the result would show only how we thought religion ought to develop. If we thought it should grow from the comparative formlessness of the Quaker to the rich symbolism of the Roman Catholic we would put the Quaker as earliest and the Roman Catholic last. If we thought the line of development was from the ornate material aids of Roman Catholicism to the pure spiritual religion of the Quaker, we would reverse the order. But as a matter of fact the six extracts might have nothing to do with real chronological growth, but might all be cut from journals that were published on the same day, coming from different backgrounds. In Palestine too there were differences of contemporary outlook represented by priestly, prophetic, and popular religion, and both the content of religion and the way in which it developed were not the same at Dan, Shechem, Bethel, Jerusalem, and Beersheba, nor among those who remained in Palestine and those who lived in exile in Babylonia. We must be prepared to find contemporary action and reaction as an aid to understanding the Old Testament.

The Bible is the record of the living experiences of a living people in contact with a living God. He revealed his will by word and deed in a historical situation, and when, later, the record was written the revelation was released from a particular time and became a timeless message to successive generations. The primary object of all religious education today, as of Bible reading, is to open the door into this Bible experience of God, so that its wealth of religious experience, the achievements of its creative personalities, and its enduring religious insight may become available to living people today; and so that the spiritual power of the same living God may be released into the modern world.

Words

Clearly it is impossible to write about theology without using words taken from ordinary human speech by which ideas are communicated, and it is necessary to say something about our use of words. If I call a rose a cabbage and spell it PRK, it does not matter so long as everyone reading PRK, or hearing 'cabbage' knows 'rose' is meant; the letters or the sound is an agreed conventional symbol to indicate a physical fact. They represent a name, and become a safe means of communication when their meaning is the same to both speaker and hearer.

But in religion words are not used always as names. When we try to express our thoughts about God, our knowledge of him or the experiences we regard as arising from meeting him, words become metaphors suggesting pictures; names of physical facts are used to indicate spiritual facts. When God is called 'father'—the father of an individual David, or a people Israel—we do not mean literally that God has a body and begets as humans do. Although the Jew believed that God had a part in all human generation and that he specially formed in the womb those who became his outstanding servants, yet it is highly probable that the Old Testament writers used the word 'father' as an image conveying all the highest spiritual elements in the relationship known as human fatherhood, without any of its human limitations. Jesus told the Jews they should show that Abraham was their father by doing the works of Abraham (John 8.39).

In theology there is a further stage in the use of words. They become a short way of referring to a whole set or group of ideas linked with the history or ritual of the past. When we say 'the blood of Jesus Christ cleanses us from all sin' we do not mean the actual physical blood that flowed from the riven side of Jesus of Nazareth in Palestine 2,000 years ago cleanses us today. We use the word 'blood' to express a complex set of ideas. In the Old Testament, which was the Bible of Jesus and his hearers, blood was thought of as the bond uniting members of a group or family, and blood rites were used to make individuals members of such blood groups; by the sprinkling of blood all barriers or enmity could be removed, and the individual then had full rights and obligations as part of the group. Sometimes God was thought of as part of the group, and an animal that belonged to him, or in some way represented him, was killed and its blood, perhaps thought of as God's blood, was sprinkled on the people to remove barriers and cleanse away separating sins; by this blood men became part of the group to which God belonged, one with God. Deuteronomy (12.23) says the blood is the life; sharing the blood means sharing the life; in Hebrew thought there was no fiction or pretence about it, it actually happened. This thought was used in the New Testament to express some of the meaning of the death of Jesus. When we commit ourselves to Jesus, his way of living, his set of values, and accept him as our leader or lord, we become part of the Jesus group. His victory over sin, his sacrifice to death, become available for us; we are 'in Christ', we have peace with God through our Lord Jesus Christ and entrance into the family that knows the graciousness of God. The blood shed by Jesus removes the barriers of sin between us and God when we are united with the living Christ by an act of commitment. It is not possible to substitute one word like 'life' or 'love' for the word 'blood' and convey the same full meaning.

In a book on the theology of the Old Testament we are attempting to convey the thought of a Semitic people who lived in Palestine about 3,000 years ago to English readers in the second half of the twentieth century. Words are used as symbols, images, and as shorthand; in a book of this size it is not possible continually to remind readers of this.

1

THE CONTENTS
OF THE OLD TESTAMENT

AN EARLY name for the whole Bible was 'The Divine Library';
some Greek writers used a neuter plural noun *biblia*, 'the
books', but the word was treated as a feminine singular by
Latin writers and the Bible was thought of as 'the book'. The
early title is useful to remind us that it is not a single book nor
the writings of a single author, but a library containing a
variety of literature written during hundreds of years by many
authors, many of whom are unknown to us even by name.
Before there was a New Covenant or Testament there could not
be an Old one, and the Jews had no single name for their
sacred writings. They classified the material into three groups,
Law, Prophets and Writings. In all the sections much is
arranged in groups of five, possibly for ease of remembering
by using the five fingers.

Law

The first five books from Genesis to Deuteronomy are Law.
The Hebrew word translated 'law' is *torah* and, whether it
comes from a word meaning to shoot an arrow or to give an
oracle, it seems to mean 'guidance' or 'direction'.[1] It is used
of the instructions given by a mother, a priest, or a prophet,
as well as by God. The difference between our concept of law
and that of the Hebrews is seen clearly when we remember that
we speak of the ten commandments, as though they are orders
forced upon us even against our will, but in the Old Testament
they are called the ten 'words'. 'Words', like prophetic words,
are a revelation of God and his will. They are his instructions
or guidance and are spoken of as his covenant. Like the vows

[1] For a discussion of the meaning of *torah*, see George A. F. Knight,
Law and Grace.

at a marriage covenant—where also the promise to obey is sometimes made—they state the terms on which life together for God and his people is possible. We should perhaps think of obligation rather than obedience, although when we are talking of God's relation with man the distinction disappears, as it did when Jesus said 'If you love me you will keep my commandments' (John 14.15, cf. 23).

Some of the law still provides the basis for our moral teaching and the deep springs whence flow—often unacknowledged and sometimes deliberately rejected—the standards of judgment and conduct unconsciously accepted outside the Bible-reading community. Even the ritual requirements, now mainly unobserved, have fashioned the forms of some Christian practices and, by typology, have determined the expression of Christian beliefs and principles.

In the Law are included the superb stories of Creation, the beginnings of human sin, and the steps taken by God to restore his estranged world to friendship with himself. There is the story of the call of Abraham and God's guidance of the patriarchs; the call of Moses and God's revelation of his personal name at the burning bush, the miraculous deliverance of the chosen people from Egyptian slavery, the covenant at Sinai or Horeb on the 'Day of the Assembly' when Israel became a people, and the journey to the fertile promised land 'flowing with milk and honey'. The framework into which the law is fitted is a succession of covenants made by God with (a) Noah, that the destructive deluge will not again sweep over the world but always the seasons will be constant; (b) Abraham, that he will have posterity and a land in which to dwell; (c) Moses first at Horeb/Sinai, containing the ten words that revealed God's requirements for his chosen people, and later in the Plain of Moab revealing the civil and religious institutions to be observed in the promised land of Israel (Deut. 29.1).

Prophets

There are two groups of material: the Former Prophets consisting of the history books Joshua, Judges, Samuel and

Kings, and the Latter Prophets, comprising the four main groups, Isaiah, Jeremiah, Ezekiel, and the Book of the Twelve —the minor prophetic books.

What we call the history books—but without the book of Ruth, which in the Hebrew Bible does not belong here—are called 'Prophetic Books' by Jews. Partly the title may be due to the theory that they were written by prophets, but clearly it is correct because they are recorded from a prophetic standpoint and with the prophetic purpose of using history to reveal God. They are not history lectures but prophetic sermons. As the Law is concerned with God's guidance and is not a textbook for general science, so the *Former Prophets* is a religious book. We waste our time and do not use the book as its writers intended if we treat it as a history book. The history is used, firstly, as incidental illustration of the faith that believed history to be the record of redemptive, righteous acts of God. The *fact of God* in history was all-important; the *facts* of history were secondary. No Jew doubted the existence of God, and the writers did not need to use history to *prove* the presence of an active God: that would have made the accuracy of the facts important. Similarly in the New Testament the all-important thing is the *fact of Christ*, the total picture, his challenge and achievements; the actual details of his life are secondary and often vague. But the history of the Hebrew past has also a vital significance for the present. Because it was a record of sin, leading to the present crisis—God's judgment proclaimed by prophets—history was important as recording, in its broad sweep, the direction in which God's purpose worked in space and time,[1] the sphere in which God's will was being achieved. Both Judaism and Christianity are historical religions, and neither Jew nor Christian would surrender the historical foundation of his religion, but the 'truth' of the Bible is not dependent on the historical accuracy of every event recorded in it.

The book of Joshua portrays a rapid conquest of all the

[1] See article by G. E. Wright in *The Old Testament and Christian Faith*, ed. B. W. Anderson.

promised land by a united people who accepted the leadership of the 'Commander' of the Lord's Hosts (Josh. 5.14), and who were ruthless in their determination not to compromise with evil. Judges tells a different story of failure and defeat; the people did evil before the Lord, forsaking him and bowing down to other gods; he handed them over to enemies so that through oppression they might learn the meaning of their sins and turn back to God (2.11ff.). The books of Samuel tell the stories of God's gift of kingship to enable his people to overcome foreign oppression, and his choice of the great David who, in later Judaism, became the ideal figure on whom crystallised the nation's hopes for God's anointed leader—the Messiah, the Christ—who would take them into the new promised land of the future golden age. David is regarded as the founder of the Temple, its music, worship and priesthood. S. A. Cook (*Notes on Old Testament History*) gave reasons for suggesting that the story of David's life has been rearranged to date all the disasters to his family and nation after his great sin against Bathsheba and her husband, and so to illustrate the truth of the prophetic message that sin and punishment belong together. The books of Kings carry the account of the results of the sins of the chosen people through the fatal schism that split north and south, to the destruction of the northern kingdom by Assyria and the southern by Babylonia.

The four works in the *Latter Prophets* record the word or message of God through the acts and sayings of chosen men who saw the events of their own times as a revelation of the requirements, judgments and promises of God. Each in his own way was called by God to proclaim a particular message, and emphasised a facet of the truth of God especially needed in his contemporary situation. We know the background of some of them, we can date them fairly accurately, and we can see how God's message through them fitted their situation. Isaiah was a courtier at Jerusalem when the Assyrians destroyed the northern kingdom and threatened the south. The book that bears his name is however composite; chapters 40-66 are not from the eighth century prophet Isaiah the son

of Amoz, and in the following pages are given the general title
'Second-Isaiah' without implying any unity of date or author-
ship. It is possible that the whole book has gone through the
sieve of the exilic or post-exilic period, during which much was
altered and added. In some Hebrew manuscripts the book
follows Ezekiel, perhaps recognising the later date of some of it.
Jeremiah also dwelt in Jerusalem but in the next century, the
seventh century BC; he came from a priestly family that lived
in Anathoth, a few miles north of the capital. A sensitive man
who shows us the deep conflicts within his own life and between him and God, he lived through the destruction of his
nation and its land by the Babylonians. Ezekiel was a younger
contemporary of Jeremiah, but was brought up in Jerusalem
and was possibly a priest in the temple there. Some of his
ministry was exercised among the exiles in Babylonia. He too
saw the fall of Jerusalem and tried to reconcile his vision of the
power of Israel's God with the destruction of God's people and
his dwelling-place in the Temple.

Amos, Hosea and Micah were all, like Isaiah, eighth-century
prophets. Amos was a casual labourer tending sheep on the
hills of Tekoa south of Jerusalem, and fig crops in the milder
climate of Samaria when the lambing and shearing seasons
finished. Although he was a southerner, all his recorded preaching was in the northern kingdom. Hosea was a northerner
prophesying to his own people. Of his life we know only the
tragic story of his broken marriage. Micah was a tenant-farmer
in the fertile lowlands that run west from the bleak Judaean
hills to the Mediterranean. He was contemporary with Isaiah,
who was prophesying in Jerusalem a few miles away, and many
contacts between the two show the same background and
reveal the fact that the knowledge of prophetic acts and words
spread through the country. But on one point their messages,
from the same God at the same time but in a different place,
were diametrically opposed. Isaiah (37.33) proclaimed that
because God dwelt in Jerusalem it would be protected and the
Assyrians would not shoot an arrow into it. Micah (3.12)
preached the coming destruction of the city; because of its sins

it would be ploughed like a heap. Isaiah's message produced great problems for Jeremiah, Ezekiel, Jesus of Nazareth and Stephen; Micah's was remembered for a hundred years and, when quoted in the trial of Jeremiah, saved his life (26.18).

In the book of the Twelve the Jewish editors put Joel, Obadiah and Jonah among the eighth-century prophets, but their introductory titles give no indication of the date when they were written. Probably in their present form they all come from the period after the destruction of Jerusalem in 586 BC. About one-third of Obadiah occurs in a slightly different form in Jeremiah 49. It is a bitter cry of exultation over a calamity that has befallen Edom as punishment for her treatment of her brother Jacob, or Jerusalem, in his hour of need. The language and content of Joel and Jonah suggest that they have passed through post-exilic hands. The former likens a severe locust plague and successive years of drought to the invasion of a northern enemy, and predicts God's intervention, the out-pouring of his spirit, and the restoration of the years the locusts have eaten. In the book of Acts (2.17) the first Christian Pente-cost was regarded as fulfilling this prophecy. Jonah is the story of a prophet of the eighth century (II Kings 14.25) probably told as an allegory in which Jonah is Israel and the great fish Babylonia (Jer. 51.34ff.), and containing a noble picture of God, the most humorous in the Old Testament, with a love that is wider than the measure of man's mind.

Nahum, Zephaniah and Habakkuk were more or less contemporary with Jeremiah at the end of the seventh century BC. Nahum gives a graphic and vivid expression of national joy at the downfall of the cruel enemy Assyria, which took place when Nineveh fell in 612 BC. Zephaniah foretells in striking imagery the coming Day of the Lord and its world judgment, when humility, meekness and truth will alone survive. Habak-kuk faces problems caused by the belief that God uses wicked people to achieve his purposes, and ends with a wonderful expression of the joy of worshipping God though all material prosperity be taken away.

Haggai and Zechariah were prophets who inspired the rebuilding of the nation and its temple after 520 BC when some of the exiles returned from Babylonia. To Zechariah has been added an anonymous section (9-14) which contains verses (11.12ff.) which the New Testament (Matt. 27.9) attributes to Jeremiah. Malachi is also anonymous; the word means 'my messenger' and in some Jewish traditions the writer is identified with Ezra the scribe.

These prophets brought a different approach to religion from the priestly attitude seen in the Law; they had a new insight into the national, social and individual requirements of a moral God. In many ways their teaching has never been superseded. S. A. Cook used to say that the real watershed in biblical religion was not the first century AD but the sixth century BC, when the religion of the previous centuries culminated in God's revelation through Isaiah 40-66, to which Jesus so often refers and by which New Testament writers expressed his significance.

Writings

The third section, probably originally called the Holy Writings, is known by the name often given in the New Testament to the whole Old Testament—the Writings or the Scriptures. It contains four kinds of literature. (a) *Books used in the Temple worship*: the five books of the Psalter, for Jew and Christian containing the classic forms of public and private devotion; it was the hymnbook of the second Temple although much of it is very much older. There are also the five scrolls used at religious festivals—Song of Songs, Ruth, Lamentations, Esther and Ecclesiastes. (b) *History books:* the two books of Chronicles, Ezra, Nehemiah, which retell the story of Israel from Adam and Eve to the fall of Jerusalem in 586 BC and continue the account through the rebuilding in the Persian period. (c) *Daniel,* which is not as in the English versions among the prophets but, like the Revelation in the New Testament, is an apocalyptic book claiming to reveal the hidden future, and in its present form not earlier than the second century BC. (d) Finally *the Wisdom Literature*—Proverbs, Job, and Ecclesiastes (which belongs here also)—books in which wise middlemen attempted to take the religion of the priests out of the Temple into the market place, and to bring the religion of the prophets down from the peaks to the plains to reach the ordinary *thinking* masses whose conduct, attitude to life, and reaction to life's problems sprang from experience rather than from dogmatic theology, priestly ritual or prophetic vision. The stress is on a man's direct standing with God.

The Work of Middlemen

The Law gives a picture of the official, institutional life of the Jew, both civil and religious; the prophetic books lift us to the lofty, often lonely, heights reached by the inspired pioneers whose visions influenced lawgivers, and modified priestly thought and practice; both were conserved and mediated by a succession of interpreters or middlemen who made them available to common people who, then as now, formed the majority of the population and who, in a later century as Mark (12.37) tells us, 'heard Jesus gladly'. Priest, prophet and middleman each had his own peculiar approach to religion and made his own contribution to theology.

The popular narratives of the Pentateuch—the first five books of the Bible in which the Law is set—were a means by which prophetic teaching was mediated to the people. Whatever their origin and date, the stories in a large measure in their present form reflect the same teaching as we find in the prophetic books. They are prophetic. In Genesis 3 sin is spoken of as disobedience to the known will of God; death means being thrust out from the presence of God who 'is thy life and the length of thy days'. God guides and moulds the destinies of nations and individuals; 'You meant evil against me but God meant it for good' (Gen. 50.20), said Joseph to his brethren. There is a covenant relationship with God apart from the great covenant at Horeb/Sinai, and God's law is in Israel's heart, almost as if the new covenant of Jeremiah 31 is interpreted in story form for popular needs, to show how it should work out in life, and to let Israel know her place in the world

God created. But the narratives are not purely prophetic. No classical prophet would have so stressed the value of animal sacrifices as to imply that the first human murder was caused by God's preference for Abel's meat diet rather than Cain's vegetables (Gen. 4.4); and there are many stories of patriarchal altars and sacrifices. Nor are they purely priestly writings. There is a distinctly popular note; it is written for and to the people. We can call the Bible 'The Book of the People', as we call the Jews 'The People of the Book'.

Another form of mediation was through the historical books from Joshua to Kings, which, as we have seen, the Jews called the Former Prophets. They are concerned to work out the prophetic teaching about rewards and punishments. God is righteous, just and all-powerful, good is rewarded and evil punished, and two sinful nations, Judah and Israel, inexorably move to destruction at the hands of Assyria in 721 BC and of Babylonia in 586 BC. The actual facts of history, the dates of the kings and all they did, were not of primary importance; continually the reader is told that if he wants facts he can consult the official day-books of the kings of Judah and Israel at the records office (cf. I Kings 14.29). The writers' concern was to illustrate the prophetic belief that history is the acts of God. In these books too sometimes the priestly point of view was mediated. Isaiah's teaching that Zion, Jerusalem, was God's dwelling-place (8.18) had led to the religious dogma that there alone could legitimate worship take place. The writers regarded all northerners, separated from the true Israel of the south and worshipping at Bethel, Dan, or Shechem, as schismatics who followed the wicked first king of the north, Jeroboam, who 'made Israel to sin' by making idols, altering the dates of the religious feasts, and making priests from common people who were not even properly ordained Levites (I Kings 12.30f.).

These forms of mediation might be called vertical. These teachers started from the prophetic height, from God. They accepted the truth of prophetic teaching and, like the prophets themselves, beginning with God they interpreted all experience in terms of the activity of God, his teaching, character and purpose. Like Hosea, they thought of the events of their life as intended by God, and sought in them a meaning that gave God's message. The fact of God was not only the basic presupposition of all their thinking, but was the instinctive explanation of all life's happenings. Their mediation attempted to bridge the gap between pulpit and pew, prophet and ordinary religious man.

There was another form of mediation: the wisdom literature that aimed definitely at the irreligious man outside the pew. Here the approach of the middlemen was horizontal. It started not from God but from common human experience, of which these wise men had intimate knowledge. Often themselves critical of both prophetic teaching and priestly institutions, they tried to help the sceptical and agnostic outsider to a new standard of values in life, a new attitude to life and to suffering. The oft-repeated refrain that runs through their books is:

> Reverence for the Lord is the beginning of wisdom,
> And to turn from evil is understanding.

Humanly speaking, the growth of Old Testament religion was the outcome of the interplay of these three types of approach to the fact of God. Continually the beliefs of priest, prophet and wise man were modified as they reacted to each other and to the popular beliefs and practices of ordinary people, and it is not always easy to discover a unity—the theology, rather than the theologies—of the Old Testament. Compared with the New Testament which may cover at the most 200 years, the Old Testament story—even apart from the early chapters of Genesis!—covers approximately 2,000 years. It is not so easy to find theological unity in the actions attributed to God during 2,000 years as in the life, death and resurrection of Jesus and a short, early period of the history of the Christian Church.

Dating the Old Testament

A wall should always be dated by its mortar, the date when it was built, not the date when its stones were formed in the

bowels of the earth or hewn from its quarries, nor the date
when the latest additions or repairs were made. However much
ancient tradition or legend was used by a compiler, there must
have been a time when each book was written in substantially
its present form. But every copy was hand-written before the
modern invention of printing. The well-preserved scrolls from
Qumran near the Dead Sea show that additions were made
between the lines and in the margins by different hands; and
the New Testament in the New English translation shows how
much different manuscripts or written copies could vary in their
contents. Additions may contain new stories or sayings, new
experiences of God that make the description of the book as
'the living experiences of a living community' even more true.
These additions may perhaps be thought of as the finger-prints
of the men and women through whose hands the book passed
during centuries. Before the book was written, the material in it
was probably passed from mouth to mouth and preserved for
generations only in retentive human memories. These oral
traditions were moulded and changed by the circumstances of
the men who passed them on. The history of the periods
through which they passed left its imprint on them.

All this makes it extremely difficult accurately to date most
of the Old Testament, or often even to find agreement among
scholars as to what is earlier or later. Perhaps we are dealing
with dry-walling built without mortar, perhaps the mortar
is difficult to date. One Jewish tradition (*Baba bathra* 14^b)
asserts that Moses and Joshua wrote the first six books,
Samuel wrote his own book and Ruth and Judges; David
wrote the Psalms with the help of the ten elders; Jeremiah
wrote his own book and Kings and Lamentations; Heze-
kiah and his men wrote Isaiah, Proverbs, Song of Songs and
Ecclesiastes; the Men of the Great Assembly wrote Ezekiel,
the book of the Twelve, Daniel and Esther; Ezra wrote his own
book and some of the genealogies in Chronicles. But there are
other Jewish and Christian traditions of the date and origin of
the Old Testament books. There are also many varying theories
held by scholars, and it is well to remember that all these

suggestions are *theories* and not proven facts. For example, some scholars claim that the one fixed date, around which all Old Testament dating can hang, was the discovery of the book of Deuteronomy in the Temple in Jerusalem in 621 BC as related in II Kings 22f. But that dating rests on the *theory* that the book of the law found in the reign of Josiah was our book of Deuteronomy. Some scholars claim that the book found was a law code now embodied in Leviticus 17-26. Others say that it was an ancient foundation document built into the foundation of the Temple and used by the writers of the book of Deuteronomy, which in its present form clearly 'spans the Babylonian exile'.

Most of those who write books about Old Testament theology accept a particular theory of the date of passages they quote. They tell us that 'this passage is clearly early' or 'earlier than' another passage. The reader should always ask 'Is there any proof of that dating?' and 'Does the dating make any real difference to the writer's arguments or his conclusions about Old Testament theology?' It is surprising how seldom the answer is 'Yes'. In this book we shall try to take the Old Testament in *its present form* and discover what is the theology of the book as we have it now.

2

THE GOD WHO ACTS

ISRAEL SHARED with other early religions the thought of God as living and active, real and present in all human life. He was known by what he did. A Jewish philosopher, Philo, wrote: 'God never ceases working; as the property of fire is to burn and snow to be cold, so the property of God is to be active and he is the origin of activity in others.' When Jesus was chided by Jews for healing on the Sabbath day he replied, 'My father is working still and I am working' (John 5.17). Although the Sabbath may have been the final act of creation, it did not mark the cessation of God's activity in the world nor of the flow of the divine energy. That energy knew not day or night, weekday or sabbath. The great creator had not retired for a rest cure but was still creating and sustaining. Whether it was weekday or sabbath the sun rose, buds burst into flower, harvests ripened, rain fell, and when a poor helpless sufferer made himself, by faith, the recipient of divine energy to heal, he did not find the power had been switched off for the day. Jesus, like the Old Testament prophets, claimed to co-operate with the ceaseless activity of the almighty God who is always, everywhere, lovingly active.

Time in the Old Testament

We have a curious way of thinking about time as though the past is behind us, the present around us, and we march breast forward into the unknown, unforeseeable future, which is in front of us but where visibility is practically nil. The Hebrew pictured himself as riding with his back to the engine, or as one of a rowing eight, not the cox. The past, he thought, lay in front of him, clearly set out for him to see, to trace its patterns, and watch the lines of its consequences running on into the present. His words for 'the early days', 'the former times', 'what happened before', are words that mean 'what is in front or faced'. The future all unseen lay behind him as he travelled backwards into its unknown regions; it was 'afterwards', 'behind'. Looking down the roads of the past, he saw not only the interplay of men and nations but he felt, with Wordsworth at Tintern Abbey,

> *A presence that disturbs me with the joy*
> *Of elevated thoughts; a sense sublime*
> *Of something far more deeply interfused*
> *Whose dwelling is the light of setting suns,*
> *And the round ocean and the living air,*
> *And the blue sky, and in the mind of man;*
> *A motion and a spirit that impels*
> *All thinking things, all objects of all thought,*
> *And rolls through all things.*

Only the perverse fool, immoral and without understanding, said to himself 'There is no God'. Others never tired of pointing to the acts of God that made the story of the past. There were patterns made by that divine activity along the walls of the past and, because God was constant, the same yesterday and tomorrow, the Hebrew believed that the lines of the patterns he traced in the past and saw running into the present continued into the future, so he could foretell the future and glance over his shoulder into the 'afterwards'. Bede drew an apt picture in his story of the conversion of our ancestors to Christianity; life to the pagan is like the bird's flight out of the darkness at one end of a lighted hall, through the hall and into the darkness at the other end. The Hebrew, standing within the lighted hall of life, tried to pierce the darkness at both ends. As he gazed into the past, the pattern of activity was clear and he adapted myths from neighbouring peoples to light up the beginnings of the story: a good creation, and the disobedience that broke the fellowship between God and man, causing the destruction of all but a righteous few. We should remember that myths are usually stories about divine beings recited at religious rituals, and to call a story a myth need not assert anything about its historicity, for it belongs to religious, not historical, literature. The problem of historical accuracy arises only when the myth is separated from the ritual and studied by itself as a story. We could say that the 'myth' of Holy Communion is the words recited at its celebration (I Cor. 11.23ff.) which Christians believe are based on a historical event. As the Hebrew, standing in the hall, looked beyond the past into myth, the bounds between history, traditions, legends and myth faded; the lines of the pattern were traced further. The darkness at the other end of the hall into the future he pierced by 'apocalyptic'—the imagination which, based on the certainty of God's steadfast continuity, enabled him to picture the future. Many writers on the Old Testament use the word 'eschatology' for this pictured future; it means the study of the last things, and comes from the Greek word, meaning 'end', used to translate the Hebrew word for 'afterwards', 'what is behind' or the 'outcome' in the future without any idea of a final end. The Hebrew word is neutral; it refers to the outcome and not an end; eschatology is a wrong word to use of Old Testament thought. For the Old Testament the dim beginnings in myth, and the future outcome in apocalyptic, blend with the present in history because they are all the acts of God through which can be traced the same pattern of divine activity.

God the Creator

We should begin our study of Old Testament theology where the book in its present form introduces its God to us, in the majestic frontispiece of Genesis 1, the picture that is intended to colour all our thought of him. When God began to create the heavens and the earth, chaos reigned, darkness covered the great abyss, and the unseeable spirit or wind of God fluttered like a bird over the waters. Then in six great acts the creative word of God went forth calling into being, first, light to break the total darkness and differentiate day from night; next the upturned bowl of the sky to break the total mass of water, holding back the waters above it from those beneath. In the third act, the lower mass of waters was gathered into one place and the habitable earth with its herbs, plants and trees stood out; then the sun, moon and stars were made to control the alternating day and night and the recurring months and seasons of the year. By the fifth word living, moving creatures were formed, swarming in the seas and flying across the face of the sky; then living, land creatures, cattle, creeping things and beasts were made to walk on the land, and afterwards, to control them all, human beings were created in God's own image. All was a good creation finished by the final act when, by a play on words, God is described as ceasing (*shabath*) on the Sabbath day.

Human, anthropomorphic, terms are used to describe the God who spoke, commanded, looked in approval on his work, and even to depict him as making man like himself. Later, when Adam begat a son, the same word is used: 'in his own image' (Gen. 5.3). Although the writer of this creation story may have used the word to indicate that he thought of God as walking upright like man on two legs, the stress is on man's authority. Man is 'theomorphic', like God, rather than God 'anthropomorphic', like man. Mankind was made like God to exercise his authority over all created beings. Personal human terms were the highest the writer knew and the obvious ones to convey his image of God. Probably for this writer as for Isaiah (31.3), although the form of God was pictured as the same as man, the content was thought of as different: men are flesh, while God is 'spirit', or breath or the powerful wind, invisible but clearly felt, known and recognised as present and active by its effect on things that can be seen. Perhaps it is a pity for our understanding of Old Testament theology and the Hebrew image of God that the three English words 'spirit', 'breath', 'wind' were all used to translate one Hebrew word. The word does not picture God as a mechanical force like the wind, but rather thinks of the wind as the breath of God, and yet links both with spirit: a word we can use for the inner essence of human life, the thinking, responsive element we include in the term 'personal'.

In the more popular story of creation in the second chapter

of Genesis, human metaphors are used even more clearly to describe the work of God. Instead of a wind blowing over the waters of chaos and an unseen God whose creative word went out, we see God moulding like a potter a clay man, blowing life-giving spirit or breath into his clay figure, planting a garden, moulding experimentally animals and birds to find a fitting mate for his clay-made man, and finally building a female form round a bone taken from the man. The same God moved about in his garden when the cool wind of evening blew, and enjoyed fellowship with his human creations until they, grasping at equality with him, disobeyed his known will, rejected his lord-ship of life, and broke the relationship (Gen. 3).

The reality behind the images, the pictures here portrayed of God, contain the three elements basic in Old Testament theology: that God is active, self-revealing, and personal. These beliefs run through the whole Bible, Old and New Testa-ments, and remain today fundamental in the Jewish and Christian thought of God.

Some writers claim that the pictures were intended to be scientific statements, but it seems more probable that their purpose was religious and that the pictures came from the words or myth that accompanied the ritual of the New Year Festival in neighbouring lands. An essential part of that ritual was the recital of successive acts of creation comparable to the six acts in Genesis 1. These acts of creation were recited and ritually remembered, in order to make the creative force work again during the ensuing year and ensure the continuance of day and night, months and seasons, the fertility of crops, cattle and children. The form of the myth or ritual is unimportant. What is important is the belief which the myth has been adapted to express; God, the great creator, made the heavens and earth and all that is therein; he has complete control of all nature; he made it and sustains it. He can destroy it or change and re-create it.

God in Nature

The primary purpose of the creation stories appears to be to relate God to history. Creation was the beginning of history when the eternal was seen in the temporal. The Hebrew word translated 'eternal' has the basic meaning 'hidden', not 'continuation' or 'permanence'. It is outside the lighted hall; it becomes seen and knowable when it is within the gleams of the light that streams out from both the open ends of the hall. But the stories stress too that God is active in nature; nature is God in action. The wind is his breath, the thunder roll is the voice of God; but he is not a nature God, he is above nature and controls it. Hebrew thought knew something of the order and constancy of nature, but it is doubtful whether there was any thought of fixed laws that limited or controlled the Creator. Man's powers of observation had not been used to classify and systematise God's way of working and to formulate unbreakable 'natural laws'. When God wished to appear to Moses he made a bush burn without being consumed (Ex. 3); to rescue his fugitive people he drove back the sea with a strong wind (Ex. 14). On the day when Israel became his people and the covenant was made, God appeared with all the accompaniment of the thunder-storm or even of volcanic eruption (Ex. 19). Often a theophany, a proof of the presence of God, was described in terms of the violent thunder-storm. Deborah waited for this proof that God has taken the field against Sisera (Judg. 5.21), and Samuel for God's command to fight the Philistines (I Sam. 7.10); Habakkuk's psalm spoke of it as the way God always comes (Hab. 3), shattering the mountains and washing the soil from the hillsides as though the hills themselves were melting.

Amos (4.6ff.) taught that famine and drought, blight and mildew, pestilence and earthquake were sent by God to win his people back, 'yet you did not return to me, says the Lord'. Through locust plague and a burning drought that seemed to devour the whole land, the prophet saw visions of God coming in judgment (7), and three verses of a hymn scattered through the book celebrate the greatness of the Creator:

Behold the fashioner of mountains, creator of spirit,
Who declares to mankind his thoughts;

Maker of dawn and of darkness,
Who treads the high places of earth;
The Lord is his name. (4.13)
Maker of Pleiades and Orion,
Changing deep darkness to morning;
Day he darkens to night when he calls the seas
And pours them over the face of the earth;
The Lord is his name. (5.8)
He makes destruction flash forth on the strong,
Like disaster he enters the fortress. (5.9)
He builds his lofty abode in the heavens
Whose arch he has founded on earth;
The Lord is his name. (9.6)

The clearest pictures of the creator God are seen in Job 38-41 and in the last chapters of Isaiah. God shows Job the glories of his world, and the beauty and greatness of God revealed through nature lift Job out of the self-centredness that had added mental and spiritual agony to his physical suffering. Isaiah 40-66 proclaim the majestic monotheism of the only God, maker and sustainer of the whole universe, but transcending nature as he transcends history. The Hebrew word for 'create' occurs more frequently in these chapters than anywhere else in the Old Testament. God is depicted as enthroned above the circle of the sky, stretching out the heavens as a tent for men to dwell in, calling out the myriad stars by name. He is the everlasting creator of the earth from end to end. He never tires or becomes weary. Though nations are as insignificant as fine dust or vapour on a balance-pan or the last drop that hangs on the edge of an empty, upturned bucket, though men are as grasshoppers or worms compared with him, yet he feeds his flock like a shepherd, carries the lambs in his arms and gently leads the suckling ewes. He opens rivers on the sand dunes and plants trees in the desert to satisfy his poor and needy. He created the earth as a habitation for man and gave its inhabitants breath and spirit. Particularly he was the creator of Israel called by his name, formed for his glory. All things were formed by him; he formed light and created darkness, made peace—the word means 'well-being' or 'whole-ness' (or good, according to the Dead Sea Scrolls, which has a different Hebrew word and sharpens the contrast)—and created evil (45.7); deliverance and righteousness come from him.

With a daring comparable with the prophecy of Isaiah of Jerusalem two hundred years earlier, this writer claims that God created the smith, his tools and weapons, and controls them all so that no weapon forged against his people can prosper (54.16). The prophet would proclaim the same faith today in an age of nuclear weapons, germ warfare and the insidious 'fifth' column activities. God controls the lips of men and speaks peace and comfort (57.19).

His creative activities did not cease at the beginning of history; he is still creating and can recreate:

> *From now I make you hear new things,*
> *Hidden things you have not known;*
> *Now they are created and not of old,*
> *Before today you had not heard of them.* (48.6f.)

He is able to create a new heaven and new earth in which joy, peace, and righteousness dwell (65); he can create a new heart, new soul, a clean heart. Throughout the prophetic writings runs the belief that the creator can make a new creation which transforms nature into harmony with the transformed humanity. The creative word that went forth in power at the beginning will continue to go forth, not returning void to God but accomplishing his purpose; instead of the thorn shall come up the cypress and instead of the briar the myrtle tree (55). The wolf will dwell with the lamb, the leopard shall lie down with the kid, the calf, the lion and the fatling together, and a little child shall lead them. The cow and the bear shall feed, their young shall lie down together and the lion shall eat straw like the ox (11, cf. 65.25).

Nature hymns in the Psalter (8; 19; 29; 65; 104; 148) lift the worshipper into the presence of the wonderful creator. They praise the majesty of God and impart a new sense of

B

man's dignity (8), the perfection of the law (19), the forgiveness that flows from the temple (65), man's confidence in God (104) and the hope of Israel (148).

The language is that of myth and poetry, not of philosophy and science. It expresses faith, a confident trust in a personal, responsive being making and controlling all things. Excavations have enabled us to recognise the imagery that came from age-old mythology in the Near East—chaos that had to be conquered, waters that had to be controlled, rivers, garden, tree of life, the serpent, the mountain of God, the first man, cherubs and precious stones. The imagery stands out most clearly in the sixth-century prophetic writings of Ezekiel (28), Isaiah 40-66 and in some of the Psalms. In Genesis it is in the background and the active God is more in evidence. This is particularly true of the mythological idea of the fight between the creator and chaos seen so clearly in Isaiah 40ff., in some Psalms (74; 104) and in the book of Job (3.8; 7.12). This idea becomes of more importance for Old Testament theology when we attempt to understand the place of evil in a God-created world. Possibly all this imagery from myth had been resisted by early Hebrew thought because of its place in the religious ritual of surrounding peoples.[1] When prophets and poets of Israel use the language and the ideas of the myths they appear to have had no fear of the danger of misunderstanding. Perhaps the influence of the myth was dead and its thought-forms remote to the circles to which prophet and poet spoke, and only the language remained as imagery or metaphor. Perhaps the situation then was comparable to ours today when we use in hymns, without realising it, metaphors from ancient Egyptian Isis-Horus cults:

> *From the overshadowing*
> *Of thy gold and silver wing,*
> *Shed on us who to thee sing*
> *Holy, heavenly love.*

In Hebrew, 'spirit' is feminine; we can use of the Holy Spirit the language of the old fertility cults, and sing with Andrew Reed:

> *May barrenness rejoice to own*
> *Thy fertilising power.*

In the New Testament the old creation stories were retold by the writer of John 1 in order to find a place, in the strictly monotheistic world of Judaism, for Jesus, to whom Christians were giving the value of God. He starts, as Genesis 1, by saying that 'in the beginning,' God expressed his will, revealed his purpose and himself, as men do, through a spoken word. Second-Isaiah (55.11ff.) depicts the word as going out from God almost in a separate existence, and John speaks of Jesus as the one in whom the word took a human form, became flesh and pitched its tabernacle among men. The bright light, that shone over the old Jewish Tabernacle, according to the stories of the Pentateuch, was the evidence of God's presence, his glory; and the light that shone from the face of Jesus was the glory of God and proved that God was tabernacling with men. The imagery of the great creator who carries his lambs in the fold of his dress like a shepherd (Isa. 40) is not far removed from the picture Jesus drew of the great God who is so much 'above his job' that he can attend to the details of human life. He knows his children's needs before they ask (Isa. 65.24; Matt. 6.32); he numbers the hairs of their head, and not a sparrow falls to the ground without him (Matt. 10.29f.). Jesus used the sustaining activity of the creator to strengthen trust in his care:

> Look at the birds of the air: they neither sow nor reap, nor gather into barns, and yet your heavenly Father feeds them. Consider the lilies of the field, how they grow; they neither toil nor spin; yet I tell you, even Solomon in all his glory was not arrayed like one of these. But if God so clothes the grass of the field which today is alive and tomorrow is thrown into the oven, shall he not much more clothe you? (Matt. 6.26)

The writers of both Testaments were struggling to express experiences too deep for words, thoughts or fancies 'that break through language and escape'. They used the only words available to them, images their readers would understand. It is not they who were 'crude'. We show our crudity when, lacking the depth of their experience and misunderstanding their poetry, we give a literal meaning to their imagery.

Breaking Fellowship with God

One of the clearest pictures of sin and its meaning in the Old Testament is found in Genesis 3. A myth of the Garden of Eden has been adapted by a great religious leader of Israel, with a keen insight into human nature and the basic truths lying behind psychology. The meaning of the chapter has been obscured by those who ask whether it actually happened or what the fruit was, and by those who build on it an elaborate doctrine of the fall of man. It is as absurd to ask whether it is a true account of a particular event in the history of the world, as it is to ask the same question about parables of Jesus; in both, the purpose of the story is to teach religious truth, not facts of history. Equally the most absurd doctrines could be formulated by emphasising particular details in Jesus's parables—his praise of the unjust steward (Luke 16.8), or the claim of the owner of the vineyard that he could do what he liked with his own, however much his action might affect other people (Matt. 20.15). So also there have been disastrous results in Jewish and Christian theology through reading into Genesis 3, with its accounts of the fall of man from a pristine state of innocence, the doctrine of the intrinsic sin of the sexual act of human conception and the transmission through it of guilt to babes unborn. The purpose of the story is to show the meaning of sin, and its origin in man's disobedience and pride. The writer believed that it was natural for God's children to live in close, intimate fellowship with him, but that always sin breaks that simple family relationship. There is no dogma of the fall of the whole human race here, and it is doubtful whether such a dogma can be found anywhere in the Old Testament. It is not *because* Adam fell, but in the same way *as* Adam fell, that the whole human race is estranged from God.

In the story Adam and his wife, settled in the garden, did not know the facts of sex, for the tree of life had been forbidden to them. The cunning serpent, symbol of the fertility deities, entered the garden and began his attack on Eve: 'Isn't it a shame that you are not allowed to eat any of the fruits of this lovely garden?' Eve bristled up in loyalty to God: 'We can eat all the fruits except one, but if we eat that God has said we shall die.' The serpent replied with one of the worst of human temptations, 'There will be no consequences', and added another temptation that even Eve could not resist, 'The fruit will make you equal with God, knowing all he knows.' She was attracted and grasped at equality with God. The tree looked good, it seemed as though it would taste good, and would make her cute, worldly-wise. As soon as she and Adam had eaten, their intimate fellowship with God was broken; they hid from him, and finally were driven out of his presence, and the guardian cherub with a whirling, fiery sword stood between them and their God. Physically they had not died, but they had lost contact with the fountain of all life.

The story puts into picture form the message of the great prophets that where there is sin there is no knowledge of God —no intimate relationship with him. Lack of knowledge of God causes people to perish, and when men choose for or against obedience to him they are in fact choosing life or death. The Deuteronomic writer stated the truth in equally emphatic language: life and death, blessing and curse, depend on choosing God and obeying him, for he is the length of your days (Deut. 30.15f.). Paul uses this picture from Genesis when, contrasting Jesus and Eve, he said that as sin came into the world when she grasped at equality with God, so salvation came when Jesus resisted that temptation and took the form of a servant (Phil. 2.7).

Disobedience spoilt the good creation, brought pain, infested the ground with weeds and caused enmity between man and other created beings. Cumulatively sin grew to jealousy, murder, and the total corruption of the universe—again some ancient myth was used to express the belief that human corruption spread to heavenly beings (Gen. 6), justifying God's drastic destruction of all but a sample remnant of every kind of living creature. Another widespread myth, or legend, of the great flood was adapted to depict the action of God, who tried in vain to wipe out evil without completely wiping out his creation, only to discover that the evil had gone too deep. Something had gone wrong with the very form of man's being, his heart (8.21). Man had to be given a new heart and a new spirit (Ezek. 36.26). Possibly in its present form the whole story was told to explain in popular form the meaning and the reason of the Babylonian deluge that swept across Palestine in the sixth century BC, destroying all but a small remnant. It expressed the teaching of the prophets that punishment inevitably follows sin, and the equally strong belief that the God who created could re-create physical nature, animals and the human heart, making a new creation.

But God is merciful, saving even the murderer from some of the consequences of his sin, which would have been as inexorable as the ancient law of blood revenge (Gen. 4.15). Sin is not inevitable. God said to Cain, 'If you do what you know to be good, will you not be accepted? If not, then sin like a wild beast crouches at your door; it wants to get at you, but you can master it' (Gen. 4.7).

God in History: The 'Righteousness' of Abraham

In the Old Testament, the darkness of the unknown period before legends or traditions began had been pierced by the stories of creation; but what they portrayed was God active in time, and throughout the book allusions to God as creator are part of the thought of God who is active in history. Creation was a work of God in history.[1] It is mentioned to strengthen confidence in his power to help Israel in the present, and to show his loving-kindness (Ps. 136.).

Jeremiah (27.4f.) said, 'Thus says the Lord of hosts, the God of Israel, it is I who by my great power and my outstretched arm have made the earth with the men and animals

[1] Köhler, *Old Testament Theology*, p. 87.

that are on the earth, and I give it to whomever it seems right
to me. Now I have given all these lands into the hand of Ne-
buchadnezzar.' Isaiah 40-66, where the creation is most often
mentioned, links it with God's call and redemption of Israel.

> *Thus says God the Lord,*
> *who created the heavens and stretched them out,*
> *who spread forth the earth and what comes from it,*
> *who gives breath to the people upon it,*
> *and spirit to those who walk in it;*
> *I am the Lord, I have called you in righteousness,*
> *I have taken you by the hand and kept you.* (42.5f.)

The prophet links the old myth of the creator's fight with the
dragon of Chaos and the drying-up of the waters of the abyss
with the holding back of the waters of the Red Sea:

> *Awake, awake, put on strength, O arm of the Lord;*
> *Awake, as in days of old, the generations of long ago.*
> *Was it not thou who didst cut Rahab in pieces and didst pierce*
>   *the dragon?*
> *Was it not thou who didst dry up the sea, the waters of the great*
>   *deep?*
> *That didst make the depths of the sea a way*
> *For the redeemed to pass over.*
> *And the ransomed of the Lord shall return,*
> *and come with singing to Zion.* (51.9ff.)

In the temple hymns, the Psalter, creation is given the same
place. It is the beginning of the story of God's acts written as
the history of Israel, just as in Genesis (2.4) it is part of the plan
of time and generations that led from the beginning through
the story of the patriarchs into recorded history.

Within that lighted hall Old Testament writers saw a wonderful dramatic story unfolding of God regaining paradise for
men whom he had created, whom he loved, chose, and to whom,
as they responded, he bound himself by covenants. The first
scenes were probably taken from Palestine's *Canterbury Tales*
—the folklore and legends sung at the sanctuaries to travellers
on the pilgrim routes to the great festivals. That the traditions

came from different groups of people is shown by the fact that Ezekiel (33.24; cf. 11.15) tells us it was the lower classes who quoted the stories of Abraham against all the best people, the 'good figs' (Jer. 24), who had been taken into the Babylonian captivity. He himself preferred the stories of Jacob to whom, in his tradition, God had given the land. The tales were woven into the stories of Abraham, Isaac and Jacob and the shrines they founded at the places where God had spoken to them. Despite their many sins—and none of them is represented as anywhere near perfect—these were men who responded to God's call and from them sprang the loved, chosen, covenanted people of Israel who believed themselves destined to spread the knowledge of God, to be his light to the world outside, the covenant bond that bound the Gentiles to him.

In the stories God is shown as calling individuals into his service to share in the fulfilment of his purpose; and he himself enters into a binding, personal relationship with men; this was the theology of the writer(s) of the stories of Abra(ha)m. The call did not wipe out human failings, but it did entail involvement or commitment on both sides.

Now the Lord said to Abram, Go from your country, your kindred and your father's house to the land, which I will show you. And I will make of you a great nation, and I will bless you, and make your name great so that you will be a blessing. I will bless those who bless you, and him who treats you lightly, I will curse. (Gen. 12.2f.)

We are told that when Abram relied on the Lord it was reckoned to him as an act of commitment or loyalty (15.6). The Authorised (King James) Version translates this response of Abram as 'He believed the Lord; and he counted it to him for righteousness.' The Hebrew word used for 'believe' is, in its simple form, used of nursing or suckling a child, and the picture behind the causative form used here is of a child trustfully, contentedly, peacefully taking food at the breast. When Isaiah (7.9) plays on the passive and causative forms of this word, the literal translation seems to be 'If you will not suck, you cannot be suckled'; unless you completely rely on God as a baby on its mother, you cannot be nourished and made strong. It is not far from the New Testament dictum 'Except ye become as little children ye cannot enter the Kingdom of God'. Abram's act of childlike trust was counted as an act that brought him up to God's standard, put him in God's group, as one with God and on God's side.

The Hebrew word translated here and usually as 'righteousness' is one of the most fascinating and important words to express the revolutionary theology of the Old Testament. In modern English 'righteousness' is seldom used outside the churches and even there it often has a derogatory sense, coming from the thought of self-righteousness, the attitude of someone who, in his own opinion, is always in the right and living by the right standard; one who, to his own satisfaction, can always justify himself. We often speak of 'my rights', a 'rightful heir', or we say 'I have a right to do this'. These all tend to be legal uses, referring to what we believe would be a favourable verdict in a law-court. They concern the demands which legally we could successfully make. But once in a Yorkshire tram I heard a child use the word in a completely different sense. The youngest of three small children had lost his penny and his elder brother, brought up to believe that if you look after the pence the pounds will look after themselves, refused to give him another. An older girl said to the elder brother, 'Give him a penny; you've a right to; he's your brother.' Here 'right' meant obligation or duty; it had nothing to do with what we mean by 'my rights', what is due *to* me so that I can demand it from others. The meaning was what is due *from* me, what others have a right to demand from me. It expressed what the brother ought to do because of a family relationship rather than because of a legal requirement. It is almost the same meaning that was given to the word by Thomas Huxley when urging the claims of the Bible in 1892:

Throughout the history of the story of the western world, the Scriptures, Jewish and Christian, have been the greatest instigators of revolt against the worst forms of clerical and political despotism.

The Bible has been the Magna Charta of the poor and the
oppressed; down to modern times no state has had a constitution
in which the interests of the people are so largely taken into
account, in which the duties so much more than the privileges
of rulers are insisted upon, as that drawn up for Israel in Deuteronomy and Leviticus; nowhere is the fundamental truth that
the welfare of the state, in the long run, depends on the uprightness
of the citizen so strongly laid down. Assuredly the Bible talks no
trash about the rights of man; but it insists on the equality of
duties, on the liberty to bring about that righteousness which is
something different from struggling for rights; on the fraternity
of taking thought for one's neighbour as for oneself.[1]

That meaning is nearer the basic idea of the Hebrew word
translated 'righteousness'; it expresses social duty rather than
legal obligation.

The fundamental thought in the word appears to be what is
congruous, fitted for a purpose, or conforming to a standard.
It can be used of telling the truth, being straight, or perfect.
When used of a sword or javelin it means 'trusty', to be relied
on to fulfil its purpose; it is often used in the Old Testament of
weights and measures as conforming to the necessary standard
(Deut. 25.15; cf. Ps. 51.19). S. A. Cook sums up the meaning
of the word when used on inscriptions as 'expressing conformity to the obligations that bind together not merely the
social unit but that organic unit of which the God also forms a
part'.[2] In that community the true member is loyal rather than
legal (these two words come from the same Latin root), and the
test of being legitimate is not legal rights but being worthy of
one's birth—the test Jesus applied to the Jewish claim to descent from Abraham (John 8.39). The Greek equivalents have
the same meaning of conformity to an established order, or,
from the standpoint of pedigree, breeding true.[3]

In the Old Testament a righteous man is one who is loyal in
his duties to his group, which includes his fellows and his God.
It is only because that was the right standard of conduct and the

[1] *Essays on some Controversial Questions*, prologue, p. 52.
[2] *Religion of the Semites*, ed. W. R. Smith, 3rd edn. p. 655.
[3] A. B. Cook, *Cambridge Ancient History*, vol. ii, p. 398.

legal requirement that the word can be treated as a legal as well as a social word, and is commonly used to describe the man who is, or deserves to be found 'not guilty'. A righteous man who had fulfilled the requirements of his community was innocent and could obtain acquittal or victory in the tribal court. Today we would not always call such a person innocent. When Judah failed to make his sons fulfil their obligations to their sister-in-law Tamar, she played the harlot, seduced her father-in-law, and was condemned to death. But when she produced his pledges and explained by whom she was pregnant he exclaimed 'She is more righteous than I'—she had fulfilled her community obligations more than he even though by so doing she had committed an act punishable by death (Gen. 38.26). So also the brothers of Joseph who had failed so miserably in their loyalty to him years before, when the divining cup had been found in Benjamin's sack, exclaimed 'What can we do to show that we are righteous?' The legal guilt was clear, the cup was found, Benjamin was caught red-handed; the problem was, what does our loyalty to the family demand from us now? (44.16).

Abram's reliance on God was treated as an act that showed him to be righteous, trusty, loyal to his obligations to God and so a member of the God-community. Basic to all Old Testament theology is the belief that God is united to, one with, his faithful people—and 'faithful' does not mean perfect, but people or individuals whom God is able to treat as righteous or trusty because of their childlike reliance on him. The necessary other side to this belief is that God is opposed to, and must in some way eliminate, everything and everyone who would harm his people; Abram's friends were God's friends and on his side; Abram's detractors or enemies were God's enemies, fighting against God, attempting to frustrate his purposes, and so must either be destroyed or made to cease to be enemies. The unrighteous man must forsake his ways or perish; a loving God cannot force obedience. In the historical writings we see this idea applied to the enemies of Israel. Some Old Testament stories depict God as commanding Israel's leaders ruthlessly to destroy his people's enemies. Some prophets foretell that God himself will destroy them; others that they will be changed, converted, or won by Israel's revelation of her God who delights not in the death of a sinner. Although the consequences of this belief probably cause more offence than any other theological concepts of the Old Testament, it is an essential element of the theology of the whole Bible—New as well as Old Testaments. The wrath of God is the necessary corollary to the love of God. His gracious mercy is part of the permanent character of God, but his wrath flashes out for a moment against all that would send a streak of evil through his creation or destroy it, or against anyone who persistently identifies himself with that evil. His constant cry is 'Turn ye, turn ye, why will ye die?'; the way is always open out of the circle of his wrath into the love of the God who is plenteous in mercy and long-suffering if the sinner will turn to him.

God in History: The Deliverance and the Personal Name

The books from Genesis to Deuteronomy tell of the growth of Abraham's family to seventy and to a great mixed multitude, during years of slavery in Egypt. Then came the gracious love that heard his children's cry for help, the power revealed in the never-forgotten deliverance wrought with mighty hand and outstretched arm against all the might of the powerful Egyptian nation and its proud king. When Pharoah, the great Egyptian ruler, had decreed that every Hebrew boy should die, God intervened, saved a baby, handed him over to Pharaoh's unsuspecting daughter to be trained so that through him God could smash that enslaving might (Ex. 1.22; 2.1.). There followed forty years—a whole generation—in the Egyptian palace, and forty as a desert fugitive till reluctantly he responded to God's call to go back to the Pharaoh with the message, 'In the name of Israel's God, let my people go'. Another generation of leading through the discipline of desert wanderings made a rebellious rabble of slaves into the people of God. At Kadesh-Barnea or Sinai or Horeb—the traditions are not clear and it is of no importance—the God who had con-

fronted Moses in the burning bush met his people and made
a covenant with them. The traditions of the content of the
covenant vary. In Exodus-Leviticus it included all the civil
and religious regulations that characterised the life of the
people after they had settled in Palestine; in Deuteronomy this
first covenant included only the ten words and emphatically it
is asserted that it included no more (5.22). The tradition known
to Jeremiah in the sixth century BC stated equally definitely that
the covenant made when God brought his people out of Egypt
consisted only of the statement, 'I will be your God and you
shall be my people' (7.23). Deuteronomy records a second
covenant containing the civil and religious regulations made
in the plains of Moab before the entry into Palestine. This may
be an attempt to reconcile Jeremiah's assertion with the traditions in Exodus, or it may represent a tradition of a two-fold
lawgiving that seems to have been known also to Ezekiel in the
sixth century BC (20.24).

For all the prophets, except Ezekiel and Second-Isaiah,
God's great act of delivering Israel from Egypt was the beginning of the nation's history and religion, although the fact
of the covenant relationship is not mentioned by any prophet
before Jeremiah. Most scholars assume that the idea of a
covenant between God and Israel as the basis of Old Testament religion goes back to Moses in the thirteenth or four-
teenth century BC, but it must be recognised that this is an
assumption and, in view of Jeremiah's emphatic statement
and the difficulty of proving any clear reference even to the
Decalogue before the time of Jeremiah, we are probably wise
not to accept the assumption without further evidence. Possibly
one group of people, such as the Rechabites who remained
separate and nomadic until the time of Jeremiah (Jer. 35) may
have been the bearers of a tradition of a covenant made through
Moses, which became dominant and national in the sixth
century. Amos and Hosea certainly knew of a close, unique
relationship between God and Israel. 'You only have I known
of all the families of the earth', God said to Israel through
Amos (3.2)—and 'knowing' meant a close intimacy comparable

to married intercourse (Gen. 4.1). Hosea, like Jeremiah and Ezekiel, used the metaphor of marriage and parenthood to express the bond between God and Israel. The first datable use of even such basic imagery as that of choice is by Ezekiel (20.5), and it was in the dark days just before the Babylonian destruction of temple, land and people—days as dark as the Egyptian slavery. Perhaps both these metaphors, covenant and choice, came into the religious vocabulary of Israel in the sixth century. But the reality they express, the close unique bond between God and Israel, appears to have been a basic element in Old Testament religion. Tradition linked that bond with the deliverance from Egypt and the formation of Israel as a nation, God's peculiar people.

The fact of the deliverance went deep into the roots of the religion. The story that Moses, like the baby Jesus, was saved from death at the hand of a cruel tyrant by the intervention of God may be a beautiful extra rather than a necessity of faith, but it is certain that the exodus from Egypt, like the Cross on Calvary to Christians, was essential to the Jewish understanding of the character of God. It was the act by which supremely he revealed his graciousness, stooping to man's need, breaking in to rescue him before there was any binding obligation.

Israel never tired of singing the song of deliverance in Exodus (15):

> *I will sing to the Lord for he has triumphed gloriously;*
> *The horse and his rider he has thrown into the sea.*
> *Pharaoh's chariots and his host he cast into the sea;*
> *His chosen captains are sunk in the Red Sea.*

The great prophet of the sixth century BC, whom we know as Second-Isaiah, found it much harder to persuade his contemporaries that the same gracious God was still active, and that his loving purpose could still be read in the story of their own day. He burst out at them, Forget the songs that tell how

> *God makes a way in the sea*
> *And a path in the mighty waters;*
> *Chariot and horse, army and power are overthrown.*

Forget these olden happenings! God is doing a new thing for you *now*, you can watch it sprouting up, or unfolding, and recognise his power in deliverance today (Isa. 43.16f.). It was a prophetic explosion. As though a Christian preacher today should say, 'Forget about the cross and all your songs of the redemption wrought on Calvary! That same God is revealing himself through suffering, death and victory today. Interpret the present in terms of the principles revealed on Calvary, so that men may recognise God active in the world now, loving and redeeming it as still he endures the suffering inflicted on him by *our* rejection. So long as there is a gap of 2,000 years between us and any recognised activity of God there will always be people who fail to think of him as relevant to daily life.'

Whatever the date of the book of Deuteronomy, the same continuing activity of the contemporary God who worked in the past and still works is seen there: 'The Lord our God made a covenant with us in Horeb. Not with our fathers did the Lord make this covenant, but with us who are all of us here alive this day' (5.2). Looking down the lighted hall of history the writer saw the ceaseless activity of God who began that intimate, saving relationship with Israel, still continuing it to his own day, and the words he used to describe it were 'loved', 'chosen,' 'covenant'.

> Behold, to the Lord your God belong the heavens and the heaven of heavens, the earth with all that is in it; yet the Lord set his heart in love upon your fathers and chose their descendants after them, you above all peoples as at this day. Your fathers went down to Egypt seventy persons; and now the Lord your God has made you as the stars of heaven for multitude. (10.14, 22)

For the lawgiver, the ritual of the sanctuary made the same assertion. Joyfully at the beginning of the harvest the Israelite took his basketful of firstfruits to 'the priest that shall be in those days' who set it down before the altar, and over the basket the worshipper saw the active, interested God approaching him down the long avenue of time:

An Aramaean wandering and lost was my father, he went down into Egypt and became a great nation. The Egyptians wronged us, humbled us, cruelly enslaved us, but when we cried to the Lord the God of our fathers he heard our voice, he saw . . . he brought us out . . . he gave us this land flowing with milk and honey. And now behold I have brought the first of the fruit of the ground which you, O Lord, have given me'. (26)

Whatever the puritan prophets might say, for many Israelites the ritual of the temple was willing obedience to the requirements of God. The food laws were a constant and public reminder that

You are a holy people unto the Lord your God and the Lord has chosen you to be a people for his own possession out of all the people that are on the face of the earth. (14.2)

The whole of the cult laws were thought of as given by God to maintain the close relationship between himself and his peoples Israel and continually to renew communion and at-one-ment.

One other occurrence in the story of the great deliverance is too important to be omitted even from a short introduction to Old Testament theology: God's making his name known to Moses.

In the New Testament there are various ways of expressing the relationship of Jesus to God, but whether we say that the Word became flesh (John 1.14), or that God was in Christ reconciling the world to himself (II Cor. 5.19), or that in him the whole fulness of deity dwells bodily (Col. 2.9), the basic meaning behind them is the same; that on an historic occasion there was revealed to man as much of God as he could understand or comprehend; that this was made known in the activity of Jesus, so that the name Jesus for Christians became the personal name for God linked with a definite historical setting.

Very much the same happened for the Old Testament when God made his name known to Moses from the burning bush, except that the name was clearly given as the name of the same God whom previous generations had worshipped under another name; no questions arose of persons in a trinity.

According to the traditions of one group, Israel had always worshipped her God under that name and shared it with all mankind (Gen. 4.26) even before she became a nation. But the dominant tradition linked the name with the historical event of the deliverance from Egypt. When God called Moses to be his agent for the great act of salvation, Moses said, 'If I come to the people and say, The God of your fathers has sent me, they will say, What is his name?' God said, 'I am who I am; say "I am" has sent you' (Ex. 3.14); and later he said, 'I am the Lord. I appeared to Abraham, Isaac and Jacob as God Almighty, but by my name the Lord I did not make myself known to them' (6.3). We do not know the origin of the name, but it appears to have been used outside Israel before Moses used it. We do not know the pronunciation of the Hebrew word translated 'the Lord' in English although there is evidence from various sources that there were long and short forms of the word, and as an element in proper names we find *Yah*, (*Y*)*Jeho*, *Jo*—Obad*iah*, *Jeho*shaphat, *Jo*nathan—which may represent pronunciation in different places. At some date Jews substituted *Adhonai*, the word for My Lord, and in English the vowels of this word were used with the original consonants to give the hybrid word Jehovah; it is possible that the original full form was Yahweh. We do not know the meaning of the word; in the verses in Exodus, by the usual Hebrew fondness for play on words, the word is equated with the simple imperfect of the verb 'to be'. From the story it seems clear that there is no attempt to explain what the word means; not *what* God is but *that* he is, was important. That he exists and is present was the sufficient guarantee that he would fulfil his intention to save his people from slavery. The name is used about 6,700 times in the Old Testament.[1] Why some writers preferred it we cannot be sure, but possibly the wise middlemen used it in their famous motto 'Reverence for the Lord is the beginning of wisdom' as a name that was more down to earth and concrete than 'God', because of its basis in history.

[1] Von Rad, *Theology of the Old Testament*, vol. i, p. 186.

God in History: Holy and Terrible

The same active God walked through the pages of the history books from Joshua to Kings. So certain were the compilers that the whole account was the story of the acts of God, that history was made to fit their vision and the books are called, as we have seen, prophetic works. Here too varying and diverse traditions were interwoven to show God in action, requiring loyalty, patiently punishing unrighteousness—conduct that failed to accord with the standard of the covenant people—teaching the meaning of sin by making its consequences clear. Most of the theology of these books arises from the work of the great prophets of Israel, who made men aware of the presence of God, taught them to see the work of God in the changing fortunes of the great leaders and of the whole nation. Prosperity was a clue to what he approved and so to his character; disaster and suffering were his punishments for sin, what he did not approve; consequences were themselves a revelation of God. But they were not thought of as the inevitable working out of laws of cause and effect, the mechanical operation of a 'power not ourselves that makes for righteousness'. They were the acts of a person; a father's dealing with his children, a husband's treatment of a loved but erring wife, a king governing his subjects.

The famous stone of Mesha, the king of Moab mentioned in II Kings 3, records that Omri, king of Israel, afflicted Moab for many days because Chemosh her God was angry with his land; later Chemosh drove out the invaders and restored the conquered territory. There is no hint on the stone that Mesha knew why his God was angry; he just was. There was not necessarily any moral principle behind the anger, it could be quite capricious. There were certain things God liked and certain he did not like; they could be discovered by trial and error, and man got on best if he did not argue but avoided God's dislikes. Like the cattle of whom Browning wrote, 'Where least he suffers, longest he endures,' so Moab viewed history and her relations with her God.

There are some stories in the Former Prophets that give the same impression: the account of the death of the man who tried to prevent the Ark from falling from an ox-cart (II Sam. 6), the vivid story of the way God enticed Ahab to his death (I Kings 22). It is possible that the sources in oral tradition or written record used by the prophetic compilers of these 'history' books were all written in this way. The national poetry book named as 'The Book of Jashar' (Josh. 10.13), the military accounts called 'The Book of the Wars of the Lord' (Num. 21.14), and the records referred to as 'The Book of the Chronicles of the Kings of Judah', may originally have been written as histories of God's actions, and not as illustrations in prophetic sermons. The lovely lament of David over Saul and Jonathan (II Sam. 1.19-27) quoted from the old poetry book says nothing of the prophetic stories of the insane jealousy of an evil king rejected by God because of his impious disobedience, nor of the close friendship between David and Jonathan that divided father and son, which helped to justify the new Davidic dynasty. A comparision of the old poem relating God's victory through Deborah (Judg. 5) with the later prose account (Judg. 4) shows some of the changes that were made by compilers; and when we read the many stories that offend against our twentieth-century interpretation of Christian standards of conduct we should perhaps regard them as coming unchanged from their source and put them into the setting of prophetic sermons, where the setting made it unnecessary to 'point the moral and adorn the tale'. The two stories mentioned above from Samuel and Kings provide good examples.

The basic meaning behind the Hebrew word translated 'holy' is uncertain, but is probably either 'to shine brightly' or 'to be terrible', giving, in the usage of the Old Testament, the sense of 'brilliance' or 'separation'. In primitive thought God's holiness was a quasi-physical force that bound together everything belonging to God, like the powerful, electric potential in a high-tension wire which, if you touch it, you cannot let go; you do not simply get a shock but you are bound to it. Holiness bound a man to God, and the emphasis is on separa-

tion *to* God not *from* the world; it made holy things belong to
God. When God first appeared to Moses in the burning bush
he said, 'My presence makes this place holy'. When God descended on to the mountain, it had to be fenced off because
contact with it by man or beast was dangerous (Exod. 19.12).
When Uzzah touched the ark to prevent it falling from the ox-
cart he was 'electrocuted' by the holiness of God, claimed by
the holy God; David did not understand, was angry with God
and left the Ark alone for three months until God showed, by
blessing those around it, that he had, so to speak, insulated it
(I Sam. 6). But one of the great prophets of Israel, Isaiah of
Jerusalem, who called God 'the holy one of Israel', broke away
from this a-moral, apparently capricious idea of holiness, and
proclaimed that God showed his holiness by loyal, righteous
acts in history (Isa. 5.16). Much later Ezekiel returned to the
old idea and decreed that priests must remove their linen
garments, in which they had ministered at the altar, before they
mingled with the people, lest the people should be made holy
and endangered by contact with the garments (44). There was,
to change the metaphor, a dangerous physical contagion about
the holiness of God which infected everyone, good or bad,
who came into contact with it. As the writer to the Hebrews
burst out, 'It is a fearful thing to fall into the hands of the living
God' (Heb. 10.31), so the Old Testament Hebrews believed that
contact with the holy God could never be treated lightly, for
he was awe-inspiring, untouchable.

Jesus appears to have used a similar idea but completely
transformed it in his high-priestly prayer (John 17.19). He had
been sent into the world, and deliberately made himself holy,
grasping the high-tension wire with one hand while with the
other he held his disciples to make them holy too, that the
current might flow through him making him the link between
them and God. 'For their sakes I make myself holy, that they
also may be made holy through the truth.' All the terror had
gone from the holiness of God, who, in Jesus, made his dwelling
with men. But neither Jesus nor his hearers were forgetful of
the importance of reverence for the holy God, the mysterious

nature of whose holy love warms man against treating him lightly.

Often in the Old Testament the word used to describe the 'mighty' acts of God in history should really be translated as 'ruthless' or 'terrible'. One of the ruthless pictures of God drawn in the Old Testament is in the story told by Micaiah of God's plans for the destruction of Ahab.

> I saw the Lord sitting on his throne, and all the host of heaven standing beside him on his right hand and on his left; and the Lord said, Who will entice Ahab that he may go up and fall at Ramoth-Gilead? And one said one thing and another said another. Then a spirit came forward and stood before the Lord, saying, I will entice him. And the Lord said to him, By what means? And he said, I will go forth and will be a lying spirit in the mouth of all his prophets. And he said, You are to entice him and you shall succeed: go forth and do so. (I Kings 22.19ff.)

Ahab had determined to go up and fight against Ramoth-Gilead, and the limitless power of God was aiding him, even enticing him along the road he had resolutely chosen to his doom. The same wind from God blows one ship to harbour and another on to rocks, in accord with the way the sails of the boats are set.

Jesus reversed the oft-repeated Old Testament picture of God as witholding rain from the wicked and sending it on the good, and proclaimed that a sign of God's perfection was that God makes his sun to rise on the evil and the good, and sends his rain on the just and the unjust (Matt. 5.45). But it is possible to see in these words not a promise but this same picture of God's ruthless use of power. God did not turn his sun and rain into weedkillers; the same powers of nature that cause corn to grow and ripen equally bring forth weeds and their seeds. If you are the kind of ass that likes thistles, then all the powers of God are growing them for you. The same power of God that helps the good, aids the unjust on his chosen road toward destruction. The love of God that ceaselessly works to save sinners, is ruthlessly active to destroy evil from the world he loves. If we identify ourself with evil, his love must become for us the wrath of God and destroy us. There is nothing capricious about his destructive wrath. It is so terrible because it is the other side of his love, and it is as great as his love. We are shocked when the Psalmist pictures God as laughing in derision at rebellious kings and rulers (2.4). When we hear Jewish historians tell us that God commanded invading Israelites to slaughter their enemies lest they should be a snare, we use this as a reason for treating the Old Testament as sub-Christian. We ignore the fact that Jesus is recorded as talking of God as the one who can destroy both body and soul in hell (Matt. 10.28) and as casting men into outer darkness where there is weeping and gnashing of teeth (8.12). For the Old Testament writers God is the *only* cause. He forms light and creates darkness, makes good and creates evil (Isa. 45.7). We do not draw the full Bible picture of God until we find room within the good and loving purpose of God for what we call evil.

3

THE GOD WHO SPEAKS

A Preface to the Prophets

IN HEBREW there is no clear distinction between words and actions. Both 'word' and 'event' can translate the same Hebrew word. Actions as well as words can speak to men, and can be used to reveal the character and purpose of God. Since often 'actions speak louder than words' the division between the God who acts and the God who speaks is partly artificial. However, in the Old Testament God was thought of as speaking in a special way through his 'servants the prophets'.

There is much that is uncertain about the phenomena of prophecy. The meaning of the characteristic Hebrew word for prophet, *nabhi'*, is not known. It may mean 'to bubble out' and refer to the ecstatic nature of prophetic utterances, or it can be derived from a word meaning to call or announce, but its form is passive or reflexive, denoting one who has been called or is announcing a message he has been given.[1] A prophet was always conscious of being used by God to proclaim a given message, sometimes about the future, more often about the past or present.

R. Pfeiffer[2] called prophecy an 'epoch-making but baffling phenomenon'. One Hebrew tradition regarded Abraham as the first prophet, another spoke of Moses as the outstanding prophet, and yet another recorded that at the time of Samuel the prophet replaced the seer, but we do not know whether these two names denote two distinct religious types.[3] It is clear that prophecy was not peculiar to Israel, but there is doubt as to

---

[1] See *Studies in Old Testament Prophecy*, ed. H. H. Rowley.
[2] *Religion in the Old Testament*, p. 83.
[3] Eichrodt, *Theology of the Old Testament*, vol. i, p. 296.

whether it was common to all the Near East and so known to Israel before she settled in Palestine, or restricted to Asia Minor, Syria and Palestine and taken over from Canaanite religion by Israel. Was Israelite prophecy ecstatic, controlled from outside, or was it an experience such as a Christian might have today? What was the relationship between the prophet and the cultus? It is probable that ecstasy, a visible, violent, emotional experience, played a part in the inspiration of some of Israel's prophets, in the way in which they both received and declared their message, and it is also clear that some of them may have been cult officials. Eichrodt suggests that prophetic ecstasy may have sprung from the group frenzy of the cultic dance, but he is in line with the modern revolt against regarding all prophets as ecstatic cult specialists.[1] For at least the great prophets the stimulus was not irrational ecstasy but the certainty of having received God's word for a particular situation, a word that came from sympathetic union with God.

Another word of introduction to prophetic theology. In our thought of time, *past*, *present*, and *future* represent distinct periods—what has happened, what is happening, what will happen. Hebrew thought was different. The perfect tense in Hebrew denotes a completed action, whether past, present, or future event so certain that to the mind of the speaker it is already completed; the imperfect tense can be used of incomplete acts in past, present and future. The divisions of time were not so definite; time flowed through past, present and future, and, standing in the present, man could be in all three divisions. Past, present and future generations were all one people. Past acts had their consequences in present and future as though the acts were still going on. Blake saw the same truth:

> *Hear the voice of the bard*
> *Who present, past and future sees.*

By the act of remembering, the covenant made hundreds of years ago became a present reality as though made 'with us today'.

[1] Eichrodt, *Theology of the Old Testament*, vol. i, p. 313.

So by a prophetic sign the future fulfilment could be made to begin now. When the prophet tore his new garment into twelve pieces he believed himself to be co-operating with the known will of God (I Kings 11.30). The future division of the kingdom had already begun in the present. God is not limited by the threefold division of time; he is in past, present and future, the unending now.

Finally, a word about the God of the prophets. Problems of conduct exist for all of us; they are part of our daily life. But when people nowadays talk about 'God' it is different. We immediately feel we have become airborne; there is nothing solid under our feet; no one has ever seen God and no one can prove that he exists. We shrug our shoulders and say with George Eliot, 'inconceivable'. Although we would not be called atheists who are sure there is no God, we are frankly agnostics who suspend judgment whether there is a 'God' and what he is like. We do not know, and in any case it cannot be proved one way or the other; God is unknowable and irrelevant for ordinary life, too remote to be the basis of our standards or conduct. We act for hope of gain or fear of consequences. Sometimes we take a longer view and think of the future of ourselves, our family, or our race. There may be a strong sense of duty, an application of some form of the golden rule: to do to others as we would like them to do to us, or so to act that we may will that the principle on which we act becomes a universal law. We seldom act as though we are in the presence of a real, living, interested God. It would probably surprise most of us to realise how few people we treat as brothers, dependent sons of the one Father.

Sometimes we find ourselves wishing there were more certainty and cry like Philip, 'Show us the Father and we shall be satisfied' (John 14.8). But we are not helped by the simple answer of Jesus, 'Have I been with you so long and yet you do not know me? He who has seen me has seen the Father.' Jesus lived so long ago, his life story is bound up with many things that seem incredible like the virgin birth and the resurrection from the dead. So we let go his simple faith in a God whom he called Father, talked to knowing he heard and spoke, treated as though he could still storms, multiply food, raise the dead: the Father to whom all things were possible. Most of us gain or regain our faith through contact with people whose experiences have made them certain of the real presence of the unseen, loving, active God seen in the life story of Jesus. A similar certainty can come from the experiences of the Old Testament prophets. They did not doubt the existence of God. Their belief, which can revolutionise our life, was that God speaks through all kinds of ordinary and extra-ordinary happenings of life. As a result he is knowable; we can worship him and co-operate with his will and purposes. Throughout the Old Testament we find men who were sure that they had met a self-revealing God who was always taking the initiative in making himself known, and who was moving forward the fulfilment of his divine purpose. When we look at the stories of these people we can discover something of what meeting God meant to them.

Many of the stories in their present form show a mingling of early traditions or ballads, and the experience of later editors who re-used them to illustrate or express the ways in which they believed God continued to speak, the message he was still giving, and the outcome of his irresistible compulsion. We shall not try to separate the old from the new, nor to date either. The first men about whom prophetic stories were told were Abraham and Moses, whose traditions are incorporated in the Law. In the history books from Joshua to Kings there was a succession of prophets from Deborah to Jonah. The stories about them show different facets of Old Testament belief in God's mode of inspiration and the ways in which men proclaimed his messages, and they prepare us for understanding the books named after the great prophets. That later hands have been at work on the accounts of both Deborah and Jonah is clear; Judges 4 is a later prose version of the old ballad in chapter 5. A comparison of the two chapters gives us valuable insight into the way the literature of the Old Testament grew, but it also shows that there was no straight line of theological development. The prose version breathes an even deeper hatred of those who, by fighting God's people, would destroy God's purposes, and sanctions as a means to God's ends the treacherous slaying of the sleeping Sisera of which the poem knows nothing. In the stories of Jonah the reverse is true. The writer of the little book has used the name of the prophet Jonah to write a story expressing an experience of God in complete contrast to that contained in Judges 4.

The First Mediators: Abraham and Moses

The word 'prophet' is used in the Old Testament first of *Abraham*. The stories of him at which we have already looked illustrate the personal character of Israel's religion and the world-wide sweep in God's promise that all nations would use Abraham's name as a word of blessing. God spoke to Abraham. There was a simple, straightforward call from God—how it came or how it was recognised we do not know, we should probably speak of an inner compulsion—to leave home and kindred and go to an unknown land. The essence of his response was what the Bible calls 'faith', absolute obedience in action (Heb. 11.8; Gen. 12). He went out not knowing where he was to go. Because the God whom Abraham obeyed responded personally to him, this intimacy enabled Abraham to be an intercessor for others. In a special way God heard him (Gen. 20.7; Job 42.8), and he became a mediator between God and man. Later prophets—Moses, Amos, Hosea and Jeremiah—all testify to the importance of this facet of prophecy which, when we make a false distinction between prophet and priest, is thought of as the function of the priest. The story emphasises that it was at the moment when he failed to trust God and stooped to mean deceit that God used him,[1] still refusing to allow the personal link to be snapped.

Both the call of God and the power to intercede are characteristic of the prophetic movement. The experience of a 'call' was the most decisive event in a prophet's life. It was an immediate contact with God which gave him his authority and his mes-

[1] C. Westermann, *A Thousand Years and a Day*, pp. 75, 210, stresses that the God of the Old Testament does not let go of those who fail him.

sage and laid on him a constraint he had to obey. Throughout his life the memory of that transforming experience moulded his ministry and dictated his message. There was no uniformity in the way the call came, or at least in the metaphors used by the prophets to describe their experiences. Some heard a voice, others saw a vision of an object, familiar or strange, others spoke of a sensation of touch or taste, but for all of them it was a clear experience they could not doubt and a compulsion they could not escape.[1]

The call of *Moses*, as we have seen, was much more spectacular than that of Abraham, involving events interpreted as supernatural. A messenger of the Lord appeared to him in a bush that kept on burning (Ex. 3). It is a pity that we translate the one Hebrew word as both 'messenger' and 'angel', and thus read into it a supernatural nuance that is not always *necessarily* present, although here clearly it is. He heard a voice calling him by name, telling him that the ground he was on belonged to God, was holy. Moses was in the presence of God, who knew the sufferings and needs of Israel and was about to intervene; he was called to co-operate in God's task of deliverance. Like many another, Moses resisted the call with familiar excuses. (1) *I am nobody:* to which God replied with a promise that rings through all prophetic experience, 'I will be with you'. (2) *I don't know you*: to which God said, 'I am the same God as your fathers worshipped, but I will give you a new experience of me, a new name or knowledge of me, a new awareness of what I am doing and so of what I am'. (3) *No one will believe me:* to which God's answer was that he would enable Moses to do deeds that would convince friend and foe of the power of his God. (4) *I am not eloquent*: to which God's answer made clear the relation between the prophet and God— I will make you a god and Aaron your brother shall be your prophet; you will put the words in his mouth and he will speak them (Ex. 4.10 and 15).

It is an excellent example of the call of God and a normal

[1] See S. Mowinckel, *Journal of Biblical Literature*, vol. 53, 1934, p. 211; J. Hempel, *Worte der Profeten*, 1949, pp. 73-189.

human reaction. Whatever the explanation of the burning bush —even an ordinary event through which a man receives what he knows to be a divine message takes on a supernatural aspect —the call was a direct encounter with God, the 'I-thou' relationship of which so much has been written by modern theologians. It brought not a deep sense of sin but a vision and a challenge, an awareness of God as personal, present, active, contemporary, concerned with his people's life, intervening to seek and save, and calling for co-operation in his saving purpose.

The stories of Moses introduce us to another word in the vocabulary of prophetic theology important in the New Testament too: *sign* or token. All the varied uses of the word can be treated as pointing to evidence that God has acted; God is already at work. Whether it refers to the future or the present, a sign gives certainty of fulfilment. 'I will certainly be with you, and the sign that I have sent you is that on this very mountain you and your delivered people shall worship me' (Ex. 3.12). The promise was already being fulfilled. God had, so to speak, put the kneeling stool on the hill and said, There you and your people shall worship. The knowledge that the stool was there remained as a permanent vision, proving that God was actually with Moses and the campaign would succeed. When Jews asked Jesus for a sign, they wanted some clear action inaugurating the kingdom of God; Jesus refused to satisfy them, but made it clear that there were signs in abundance for those with eyes to see them (Mark 8.12).[1]

Another story emphasises God's unique treatment of Moses. To other prophets God makes himself known through an appearance—a vision or reflection in a mirror—and in dreams. But to Moses he speaks mouth to mouth, openly not in riddles or parables, so that he sees the likeness of the Lord (Num. 12). The meaning of the metaphors is not clear, but they stress degrees of intimacy between God and man, varieties of religious experience amply attested by history.

An interesting metaphor is used to express the fact that the

[1] A. M. Hunter, *Introducing New Testament Theology*, p. 29.

pattern of God's activity is more clearly discernible in the past than in the present: the story of Moses hidden in the cleft of the rock, unable to see the face of God but only his back when he has passed (Ex. 33.23). God is revealed by what he has done. So Elijah in the same rocks saw the effect of God passing but heard him only in the final act (I Kings 19.11).

Throughout the stories of Moses, elements from his call vision were decisive. The *holiness* of God pervaded the whole Horeb/Sinai narrative. There was a *personal* relation with God through which knowledge of God was communicated and his word proclaimed. Awareness of the real *presence* of God in ordinary life was the inspiration of Moses, as was his belief that Israel was *God's people* to whom he revealed himself in a special intimate way. All this made Moses, in Israelite tradition, the founder and mediator of the covenant.

Early Messengers: From Deborah to Jonah

Although according to the writer of Deuteronomy 'there has not arisen a prophet since in Israel like Moses, whom the Lord knew face to face' (34.10), yet stories in the historical books from Judges to Kings show that the stream of prophetic religion flowed unbroken to the emergence of the great prophetic figures of the eighth century BC. The book of Judges tells of *Deborah* the prophetess, a spirit-filled judge and leader, who like Miriam had the power to celebrate God's deeds in song and to see in historical events the acts of God (Judg. 5). Her call was to inspire a military leader to co-operate with God in fighting his people's foes at a time when the nation had either to fight or perish. As to many prophets, her call came through a historical event, a national crisis, interpreted as the moment when God had decided to intervene to give his people victory. In poetic language she pictures the mighty God of battles using all nature—thunderstorms and the stars in their courses—to defeat the enemy. To her, God was a jealous or zealous God; the two adjectives translate one Hebrew word, and both in English come from the same root indicating a deep emotional commitment. The vivid poetry of the song was misunderstood by the writer of the parallel prose version (Judg. 4) who attributed to Jael a treachery absent from the older poem. But the writers of both poetic and prose versions give a picture of God in complete contrast to that in the book of Jonah. They were living in the midst of a life-and-death struggle where compromise meant destruction. Israel's enemies would crush her, prevent her obtaining the promised land; they were God's enemies and must perish. There was no vision of any other way of destroying evil and fulfilling God's purpose except the destruction of evil-doers,

> *So perish all thine enemies, O Lord!*
> *But thy friends be like the sun as he rises in his might* (Judg. 5.31).

Some of the stories of *Samuel* show him as a prophet called to be a national leader against foreign oppression, but he recognises that the evil which God is fighting can also be within his own people, its priests and its rulers. In this he is linked more closely with the great classical prophets of a later century.

As a child he was dedicated to the temple service at Shiloh, and from being part of the temple personnel wearing the priestly linen ephod, he was called by the voice of God—an audition not a vision—to be a prophet at a time when the word of God was rarely heard, his visions seldom seen, and when Samuel himself had no experience of God. The message came in a dream announcing God's doom about to fall on the priestly house of Eli. His reputation as a prophet grew, all his predictions were fulfilled, God continued to appear to him in messages, and like Moses he proved his prophetic calling by his faithfulness (I Sam. 3.20). In later tradition, Samuel and Moses were spoken of as outstanding intercessors (Jer. 15.1). Samuel belonged to the period before religious leaders—prophets, priests, judges—were differentiated. He called the nation to repentance (I Sam. 7.3). He offered sacrifices to gain God's intervention in battle against the Philistines (7.10). On annual circuit he performed the duties of a judge (7.15). He anointed kings to follow him (10.1). He was a clairvoyant who for a fee discovered the whereabouts of lost asses (9.7), and was leader

of a group of ecstatic prophets living together as a community
(19.20). Possessed by the zealous spirit of the Lord, he hewed
king Agag to pieces before the Lord (I Sam. 15.33). But in his
doom on Saul he proclaimed a religious message comparable
to the words of the great prophets and Jesus:

> Has the Lord as great delight in burnt-offerings and sacrifices,
> As in obeying the voice of the Lord?
> Behold, to obey is better than sacrifice
> And to hearken than the fat of rams.
> For rebellion is as the sin of divination,
> And stubbornness is as iniquity and idolatry.
> Because you have rejected the word of the Lord
> He has rejected you from being king. (1 Sam. 15)

The religious experiences of *Saul* were similar to the ecstasies
of Moslem dervishes and some Christian sects today. He was
chosen by God and anointed by Samuel to be national leader to
save Israel from her foes, and it has been suggested that this
type of ecstasy arose from the contagious excitement of the
holy war. Signs were given to Saul to prove that God had acted
and was with him in his fight. When he met a band of ecstatic
prophets inspired by music, the spirit of the Lord entered him,
and so completely changed him into another man that on-
lookers, surprised at the change in an ordinary young son of a
farmer, uttered a cry that became a proverb, Is Saul among the
prophets (I Sam. 10; 19.24)? Later it was an evil spirit from
the Lord that entered him, made him 'rave' and try to murder
David (I Sam. 18.10). Often we find madness and prophecy
linked. Even Jesus was said to be 'beside himself' (Mark 3.21).
Any extraordinary enthusiasm or powers were thought of as
from God and could be directed by man to his own ends,
either the destruction of himself or of evil. One story of the
way Saul received inspiration tells how he sent three successive groups of messengers to a prophetic encampment pre-
sided over by Samuel. Each group was seized by spirit contagion, and finally Saul arrived at the encampment, prophesying
as he went, stripped off his clothes and lay naked all one day
and night (I Sam. 19).

The accounts of Saul's experiences have led some scholars[1] to suggest that Israelite prophets, like Canaanite prophets of Baal, were organised in communities closely linked with shrines and there is support for this suggestion in some of the stories of Elijah and Elisha. Mowinckel[2] claimed that Psalms in which God speaks in the first person contain prophetic utterances giving the 'Thus says the Lord' reply on a particular cultic occasion. Prophets were seized by ecstasy and filled with supra-normal divine power during the orgiastic tumult of great cult festivals. So far as Saul is concerned, there is little evidence of connection with shrines or cultus, and no prophetic messages by which he can be judged. We know much today about the emotional tension that produces the ecstatic type of religious experience, but the criteria by which we judge its theological value are not much different from those laid down in Deuteronomy—the content of the revelation, the direction in which it leads men (chapter 13), and its outcome in history (chapter 18). Contact with God should produce something valuable and Godlike. There is necessarily emotion in every religious experience, but a full experience should involve the whole man —thought and will as well as emotion—and we are right to distrust emotion that does not issue in character and action comparable to the character of the God who is credited with inspiring the emotion. The ancient Hebrew believed that human life was open to the influence of spirit forces from outside. The unseen spirit world is not so real to modern man and he has other theories to explain his conduct. We still use the metaphor of 'inspiration,' but we are told that the Hebrew belief is inconceivable in modern civilised societies because science has ruled out the possibility that the divine spirit can physically enter a man, and because our notions about processes are different from those of the ancients. Perhaps modern psychological theories may prove accurate; perhaps the ancient Hebrew theory of the direct impact of Spirit on spirit may have truth in it. At least if we are to understand Old Testament theology we must appreciate how the Hebrew mind worked.

[1] Hölscher, *Die Profeten*, 1914.   [2] *Psalmenstudien*, vol. iii, 1923.

C

Nathan foreshadows the classical Hebrew prophets in his moral message and his political activities. He first appears as an official court prophet (II Sam. 7.2) consulted by David when he wished to build a permanent 'house' for God, his immediate reply being of consent and approval. But that night Nathan had second thoughts. The Word of the Lord came to him reversing his decision. God would establish David's seed as a permanent 'house', but the Lord's house must be built by David's son. Clearly, a prophet could speak out of his own heart a message which did not coincide with the will of God and which had later to be corrected.

Nathan is known better for his famous rebuke of king David for his relationship to Bathsheba and her husband Uriah (II Sam. 12). The story was probably told by women singers quite as interested in the fascinating beauty of a queen who wielded a powerful influence as in the moral aspects. David married to many women, saw the wife of one of his army officers, who was away on active service, bathing within sight of the palace windows. She was not averse to accepting a summons to the palace and its harem, and after adultery the king tried various ways of deceiving the husband when she knew she was pregnant. They were unsuccessful, and we watch the officer returning to his unit with his own death warrant—a sealed letter from David to the officer commanding telling him that Uriah must not be allowed to return home alive. Nathan's parable seemed harmless; the poor man's one lamb that had grown up with his family was taken by the rich man, who spared his own large flocks, to provide a meal for a guest. David's judgment on the rich man was met by the prophetic 'You are the man'. The prophet's message was prefaced by 'Thus says the Lord, the God of Israel, why have you despised the word of the Lord to do what is evil in his sight?' It is a clear statement of one main element in prophetic theology, the belief that God is concerned with human conduct. Stealing, killing, adultery, coveting (the word means to desire, take steps to obtain) a neighbour's wife are crimes not only social but also religious. Other prophets condemned adultery; lawgivers

(Deut. 22; Lev. 20) made death its penalty, and there was equal payment for men and women. Adulterers were outside the covenant (Ps. 50); it was sinning against the light (Job 24). In the New Testament it heads the list of the sins of the flesh (Gal. 5), excludes from the kingdom of God (I Cor. 6), and is a crime against the second great commandment, 'You shall love your neighbour as yourself' (Rom. 13). It is a sin against God in both Testaments. It shows lack of the Godlike character of righteousness or loyalty.

In Bible faith, husband and wife were created by God as one flesh, and whoever puts away husband or wife and remarries commits adultery. Sexual morality and the right use of our bodies is a primary demand and basic to the fulfilment of the divine law of love. The faith of the Bible is not remote from daily life. Adultery disintegrates the community, smashes social life, makes family life impossible and ruins the lives of children; unforgiven adulterers, according to the Bible, have no part in the Kingdom of God. When the happiness of a second marriage is cited as proof of God's blessing on divorce,[1] one is inclined to ask whether this self-centred judgment applies 'until seventy times seven' and whether God's condemnation is not revealed in the unhappiness of discarded partners and children.

Another prophet now introduces us to a new element, prophecy by action. During the reign of Solomon, *Abijah* of Shiloh instigated to revolt an able youth whom Solomon had put in charge of forced labour in the northern part of Israel. The prophet tore his own new garment into twelve pieces and gave ten of them to Jeroboam saying, 'Take for yourself ten pieces; for thus says the Lord, the God of Israel, Behold I am about to tear the kingdom from the hand of Solomon and will give you ten tribes.' The action was not symbolic but functional; it made the prophecy begin to come true. The action differed from that of a witch doctor who seeks to coerce God to do man's will; it co-operated with the previously revealed will of God and made that declared will begin to be fulfilled (I Kings 11.31).

[1] *Objections to Christian Belief*, 1963, p. 14.

In Hebrew thought when the word of God or his messenger had been spoken, something irrevocable had happened: it would not return empty. But when the word was supported by prophetic action, the fulfilment had already begun to take place. Such actions were dangerous, for apparently this co-operation released the power of God. Later we find this same prophet jealous for the righteous sovereignty of God, condemning Jeroboam and supporting revolutionary dynastic changes. For Abijah as for Nathan there was an external authority by which kings as well as people were judged, a personal power, greater than earthly monarchs, enforcing religious and moral standards.

The story of the death of Elisha (II Kings 13) contains another example of functional prophecy. With the prophet's hands laid on the king's hands the king shot an arrow through the window ensuring victory, but because he beat the ground only three times the king could defeat the enemy thrice only. In the books of Isaiah, Jeremiah and Ezekiel there are many more examples of such prophetic functional acts. It has been suggested that three great final deeds of Jesus were acts of functional prophecy. Riding in triumph into Jerusalem actually inaugurated the Kingdom. Cleansing the temple purified worship. The last supper began, and gave meaning to, the sacrifice on Calvery.

The stories of *Elijah* and *Elisha* continue to show God's demand for moral standards, and his judgment on rulers. But there is a new emphasis on the choice that must be made between the true God and false gods, and on miracles which have close parallels with the gospel stories of Jesus. In both there is raising the dead, cleansing lepers, multiplying food, controlling nature so that an axe head swims or a man walks on water, wonderful happenings on a mountain top, a mysterious ascension into the heavens, and the hope of a 'second coming' (Mal. 4.5). Historically and theologically the stories belong together, and it is understandable that some contemporaries regarded Jesus as a second Elijah.

A three-year drought, interpreted as God's judgment on a

sinful nation, brought Elijah into Palestine wearing the professional garb of a prophet, camel-hair mantle and leathern girdle (II Kings 1). In a dramatic act on the top of the Carmel range he proved that his God controlled nature, giving rain and fertility, and he slaughtered four hundred rival prophets who were leading the nation astray. The ringing challenge to choose the Lord or Baal (I Kings 18.21), highlights for the writer the conviction that in our choice of a god lie the issues of life and death (cf. Deut. 30.15ff.). But the act by which he was chiefly remembered was his championing in God's name of a smallholder whose land was adjacent to king Ahab's palace (I Kings 21). Naboth refused to sell his vineyard. 'The Lord forbid that I should give you the inheritance of my fathers.' Ahab, knowing the sturdy Israelite independence and the limits of a king's power, accepted the decision, turned his face to the wall and sulked. Jezebel his queen, brought up in another tradition, borrowed the king's seal, and had Naboth accused of treason, falsely condemned and stoned. His property, including the vineyard, was forfeit to the king. Ahab leapt from his bed, walked through the palace grounds to take possession of the coveted vineyard, but found Elijah leaning over the gate waiting for him with a message from God. 'Have you killed and also taken possession? In the place where dogs licked up the blood of Naboth shall dogs lick your own blood,' and as for Jezebel, 'dogs shall eat her within the bounds of Jezreel'.

Something of what the stories of Moses and Elijah meant to Jesus is seen in the account of the Transfiguration (Matt. 17). Both these men had been excluded from the promised land, dismissed from God's service because in face of the threat of death they had lost their trust in God (Deut. 32.51; I Kings 19.16) but Jesus was transfigured by a deeper trust that enabled him to set his face like a flint to go to Jerusalem and death (Luke 9.51).

Another prophet, *Jonah*, mentioned in the book of Kings, is important for Old Testament theology (II Kings 14.25). He was a nationalist prophet who inspired Israel's king in his successful fight to regain territory from Syria. He proclaimed God's mercy on Israel, and he lived when the cruel, barbarous

Assyrians were beginning the conquests which destroyed the kingdom of Israel. He is important because hundreds of years later a writer used his name for a parable or allegory containing one of the loftiest pictures of God in the Old Testament—the God who cares for all men, even if they are so reprobate and wicked as the inscriptions in the British Museum prove the Assyrians to have been. Ordered to preach against the wickedness of Nineveh, capital city of the Assyrians, Jonah fled in the opposite direction, but, miraculously brought back by God, eventually he obeyed. So effective was his preaching that the whole city repented; king and people and even all the animals fasted and wore sackcloth—a lovely picture! Jonah was very angry with God for being gracious, full of compassion, and plenteous in mercy toward such evil people. The book ends with God's twice-repeated question 'Are you very angry, Jonah?', the growth and withering of the shady gourd, and God's final plea on behalf of 120,000 innocent babies in Nineveh 'and also much cattle'. It is the strongest and most humorous plea in the whole Bible for missionary activity, for overriding all national boundaries, and for belief in the wideness of God's mercy toward even the most justly hated people. It contrasts the greatness of God's love with the narrowness of man's forgiveness; the God who sends his prophet to seek and save the cruel, ruthless oppressors of his own people; and the prophet who refuses to go lest they shall repent and escape the destruction they so richly deserve. The book of Jonah breathes a world-wide sympathy and tolerance which, like the similar, lovely book of Ruth, may have been a counter-blast to rigid, exclusive nationalism. It ends our survey of these eight early messengers with a theology in complete contrast to that of Deborah, with which we began.

God Speaks in a Crisis

Now we are moving towards the crisis of the prophetic movement. 'The prophetic life was lived, and the thought of the prophets developed, under the impact of a new reality which menaced both their own personal life and that of their nation.'

So Professor Eichrodt writes.[1] The experience of a call brought a new certainty of the reality of God, the inevitability of the clash between God's will and the direction in which the world was moving. A compelling, irresistible power smashed the whole previous pattern of their lives, forcing these prophets to testify to an imminent, threatening, divine irruption into individual, religious, national and international events. The drift away from God and the elaboration of religious ritual divorced from moral life, wide-spread sexual immorality, selfish overreaching greed preoccupied with material gains, senseless luxury, injustice and oppression, the rise of ruthless, powerful nations—all these things must, unless there was a complete change and a turning to God, bring again the destructive deluge of divine wrath. The prophets saw the dark storm clouds gathering, they heard the voice of God in the rumbling thunder of hostile armies on the move proclaiming with terrifying insistence, 'Prepare to meet your God.' God's voice spoke to a chosen people who, rejecting all his loving pleading, persisted in lying, rebellion and treachery. As later Jesus weeping over the doomed Jerusalem cried 'How often would I have gathered your children as a hen gathers her chicks under her wings, but you would not' (Matt. 23.37), so Ezekiel in the sixth century called the people to turn: 'why will you die?' (18.31). This was no working of a mechanical power, an impersonal force of fate. It was the suffering of a father whose love has been rejected and who is unable to save his children from self-destruction.

But before we look at what the classical prophets said about the crisis around them, we should ask how God spoke to them. Was the mode different from that usual today? Or were only the theories about God and man different then, so that men expressed their experiences in different metaphors? In the New Testament it is stated that all scripture is inspired by God and that God previously spoke in fragmentary ways through prophets but now through a son, that in Jesus the word became a human form—as in the Old Testament we are told that the spirit of the Lord clothed itself with Gideon. Brunner wrote of

[1] *Theology of the Old Testament*, vol. i, p. 345.

prophetic ascription of words and statements to God as 'an Old Testament level of revelation'. When a prophet prefaced his message with 'Thus says the Lord' or 'The word of the Lord came to me' did he mean that the actual words he used were given to him by God? In the New Testament the disciples were told that when they were arrested they should not be anxious what they should say 'for what you are to say will be given to you in that hour; for it is not you who speak but the Spirit of your Father speaking through you' (Matt. 10.19f.). Some prophets might have believed that God spoke through their vocal chords, others that the words in which a prophecy was expressed came from God, rather than, as we might say, that a thought, or a conviction that sprang from reflection, was inspired by him.

It is agreed that the ultimate ground of prophetic experience was the belief that God speaks in a way man can understand. Even if we discard their language of physical sensation to express that experience, the experience itself has not vanished, and we need to ask whether it is still available. We do not know when, in Bible religion, the literal use of language became conscious metaphor; we still use the phrase 'inspired by God' without making clear that we have passed from literal to figurative usage. With all the aids of modern science it is not easy to find language to express our experiences, nor to explain the source of voices and visions, the flash of a new idea, the fresh meaning of a familiar saying, the sudden message from some common scene. The more aware we are of God, the more we are likely to say:

> And every virtue we possess
> And every victory won,
> And every thought of holiness
> Are his alone.

Because we have no other language in which to express this utter dependence on God, we retain their well-known metaphors to communicate prophetic experiences, which they interpreted as evidence of direct personal contact of spirit with

Spirit, and which can all be paralleled in later religious literature.

As we try to discover the theology of the classical prophets and pierce beyond their language to their experience, two facts are important to recognise. The first is that God's message was always to an individual in a particular place, time, and set of circumstances so that it was coloured by personality and background. Bishop Phillips Brooks said that preaching is truth through personality. Shelley put it,

> *Life like a dome of many-coloured glass*
> *Stains the white radiance of eternity.*

The truth from God came through the coloured glass of the individual prophet, we cannot generalise it and apply it to everyone, everywhere, always. Before it can become God's message to us, here and now, we must try to get a glimpse of the 'white radiance', the word of God that comes through the Old Testament. Paul described Christians as those who were led by the spirit of God (Rom. 8.14), and Jesus promised fuller revelation as we are guided into all truth by the same spirit (John 16.13).

The second fact is that God used the *whole* personality of the prophet; he was a personal agent not an unconscious instrument, an ambassador not a postman. Human powers were not merged or absorbed in the divine. Moses and Jeremiah could hold back and remonstrate when called; like Amos they could turn on God in intercession or protest. The utterance was not an enigmatic, mysterious saying that had to be interpreted, it came through the prophet's own consciousness and it was the prophet who was inspired rather than the word. This did not mean that the prophet could choose whether to deliver the message. The confidence behind his 'Thus says the Lord' was the certainty that he had been irresistibly seized or arrested, made to reveal the divine will. The message was not his own nor was it presented as new or original. The moral code was known; it was an accepted way of life that the priests should have been teaching and the people observing. Even phrases from the messages of contemporary popular prophets were picked up and emphasised. 'You are saying, "God is with us", and he really will be if you fulfil his demands' was proclaimed by Amos (5.14), Micah (3.11) and by Isaiah in his famous 'Immanuel' passages. The God proclaimed by the prophets from deep personal experience was not an unknown God but one who had been in living relation with Israel for centuries, and whose requirements had been handed on by prophet, priest and parent. What distinguished the Hebrew prophets was not the novelty of their teaching but their clear, vivid awareness of the *fact* of God—his presence, demands, judgments, and saving activity. This changed their own lives and made them apply the age-old truths to their own situation, producing what it is fair to call the prophetic religion of the Bible.

The Rod of Assyria: Amos, Hosea, Isaiah, Micah

Amos, a casual farm worker from the hills of Tekoa in southern Palestine, migrated to the luxurious royal shrine at Bethel in the north, became a dangerous preacher of the righteousness—the standard of loyal conduct—required by God, and was driven out by the high-priest lest he caused a revolution. He prefaced each sermon with a startling text in memorable poetry (1.2; 3.1f.; 5.2). Because

> The Lord roars from Zion,
> And utters his voice from Jerusalem,

he condemned surrounding nations for inhumanity, and then turning on his hearers, denounced them for worse crimes against man and God. To a people conscious of their privileged relations with himself God says,

> With you only have I been intimate
>   of all the families of the earth;
> Therefore I will punish you
>   for all your guiltiness.

God is working, foreign armies are approaching who will leave only a remnant as small as a couple of chewed legs or a bit of an

ear of a lamb torn from the mouth of a lion (3.12); a violent
end is coming on elaborate altars, luxurious houses (3.14f.),
sleek senseless women—a prize breed of fat cows—who oppress
the poor and crush the needy and say to their men, 'Come on,
let's have another drink' (4.1), the worshippers who show their
rebellion against God by gathering at the churches of Bethel
and Gilgal to offer their annual sacrifices every morning, their
triennial tithes every three days, and put their names at the
head of published subscription lists (4.4f.). God has sent
famine, drought, blight, war and earthquake to show them the
meaning of their sin, 'Yet have you not returned to me'; and
now God is about to confront them in a way they cannot
escape, 'Prepare to meet your God' (4.12).

In a wailing song—used in ancient days to conquer foes by
treating them as ready for burial—he sings,

> *She is fallen no more to rise,*
> *The virgin of Israel;*
> *Forsaken on the ground,*
> *None raise her up.*

Only a tenth will remain, because Israel had sought religious
institutions and not God; they have hated justice and trampled
on the poor; they have prayed for God's intervention to help
them—the day of the Lord—but when the righteous God comes
it will be in judgment. He says:

> *I hate, I despise your feasts,*
> *And I take no delight in your religious festivals.*
> *Take away from me the hubbub of your hymns*
> *To the bellowing of your organs I will not listen.*
>
> *Let justice roll down like water*
> *And righteousness like a perennial stream.* (5.21f.)

Amos (7) tells of the way God called him, seizing him as he
followed the flock and compelling him to preach; of the
locust plague and devastating drought that made him plead
with God to forgive, to stop punishing Jacob because he was
so small; of the plumbline showing that the whole nation was

dangerously out of true like a wall shaken by a great earthquake; of the basket of summer fruit which, by a pun on their
name, spoke to him of the end (8.1f.); of the ruined temple
with its broken pillars and fallen roof that had crushed the
congregation (9.1ff.). All proclaimed the same message that
though men dig down to hell or climb into heaven they cannot
escape from God.

Like the other prophets of the eighth century, he blew sky
high the structure of contemporary religious life by proclaiming
that God is more interested in right human conduct, a right
attitude to our fellows, than in ritual and religious ceremonial,
however costly, beautiful or elaborate. The content of worship
and adoration is not exhausted by kneeling in cloistered beauty
contemplating the holy God, or giving material possessions as
sacrifices to him or his church. Embodying in daily life the
character of God is itself an act of true worship, not simply an
outcome of worship. Amos was the first prophet to teach history from an international—or supernational—angle. His was
not from the 'favoured nation' standpoint which habituates us
to think primarily of our own country, its victories and defeats,
whether right or wrong. He thought in terms of God, his purposes and standards. Amos did not think of a totally detached
God who treated all nations the same whatever their stage of
development or national potentialities; Israel was a privileged
people, but that brought an equal measure of responsibility.

It was his marriage that *Hosea* interpreted as God's call.
Either he fell in love with and, as a dramatic prophetic action,
married a known prostitute or, more likely, the woman he
married became unfaithful. The names of the three children
suggest that none of them was his. The marriage may have
endured till the children were old enough to plead with their
mother to be faithful; she may have left him, been sold into
slavery and eventually been bought back by Hosea. The details
of the story have become so interwoven with teaching and
allegory that they cannot be reconstructed with certainty, and
they are of little importance. What is clear is that this broken
marriage was a personal experience he felt on his pulses. It

was *his* home that was involved and the woman he loved with every fibre of his being; and his description from inside of the rottenness of the religious life of Israel throbs with the agony of personal experience. For him the cause of the nation's condition was not unrighteousness in social life, but immorality within the religious life. Amos had said that ritual was no substitute for morals and had nothing to do with the worship of Israel's God; Hosea called ritual apostasy, treachery, whoredom and adultery. People might think they were worshipping the Lord under another name when they used the name *Baal*— Lord or Husband—and took part in fertility ritual, but in reality they were worshipping another god; it was Canaanite religion and a relic of heathenism. Perhaps there was something of the attitude of the Puritans who refused to celebrate Christmas because the date linked it with a heathen festival; perhaps Hosea condemned a religion similar to the religion of those today who, making their aim wealth, fame, or self-centred advancement, continue to take part in Christian worship thinking they are followers of Jesus of Nazareth, while really worshipping other Gods.

Amos had begun by pleading and intercession, but was later forced to stand with God and accept the inevitable necessity of impending doom; Hosea never seemed willing to accept it. A vivid, surprising feature of the book is the sudden introduction of a promise of hope to balance a threat of destruction. So abrupt is the transition that sometimes, from a literary standpoint, the promises seem to be later additions, but religiously and psychologically the alternating of despair and hope, doom and promise, is of the essence of the prophet's struggle against the habitual fatal sin of the wife he loved. The conflict was within his own heart. His love for Gomer was something he could not kill: it was a covenanted, bound love; and he believed God stood with him as husband and father bound to treacherous Israel and crying,

> O Ephraim how can I give you up,
> How can I let you go? (11.8)

Hosea's own bitter experience enabled him to understand something of the unchangeable, limitless, forgiving love that bound God to his people, the suffering of rejected love, and the hope that, when war had swept away her material prosperity and all the false religious ritual, in the simplicity of the wilderness she would respond to him as in the days of her youth (2.14).

To Hosea the basic sin of Israel was that she did not know God—had no intimate fellowship with him, and so there was no faithfulness or kindness but swearing, lying, killing, stealing, committing adultery; all bonds were broken and murder followed murder (4.1f.). The disorders in social life were found in religious life too, where priests were as bad as people, and in political life with its frequent murders and senseless rushing for foreign aid to one country after another without any reliance on God (7.11). Israel's repentance was superficial, it vanished like morning dew at sunrise (6.4). There was no sense of guilt and God was thought of as easy-going, as to many Christians who stress only the love of God: they said there was no need to worry 'as soon as we seek him he will turn and we will find him'. Punishment became a horrible necessity to show the intrinsic nature of evil.

The characteristic word used by Hosea of God is translated 'loving-kindness'. It is a good translation if we remember that 'kindness' is linked with 'kith and kin', and is the loving relationship we show to those who are bound to us by ties of affection and kinship. It stoops to needs when no rights can be claimed; our needs become our rights. While we are still sinners he comes to our aid. Loving-kindness becomes, in the New Testament, the grace of our Lord Jesus Christ, the attitude of the Father who so loved that he gave. God requires from his true worshippers the same attitude.

> *I desire loving-kindness not sacrifice,*
> *The knowledge of God rather than burnt-offerings.* (6.6)

The first five chapters of the book of *Isaiah* summarise the prophet's teaching, and show the same theology as in Amos and

Hosea. The father's cry for what used to be called 'piety' is the same:

> *Hear, O heavens and give ear O earth;*
> *for the Lord has spoken:*
> *Sons have I reared and made great,*
> *but they have rebelled against me.*
> *The ox knows its owner,*
> *the ass its master's stable;*
> *But Israel does not know,*
> *my people does not understand.* (1.2f.)

His condemnation of all the sacrificial ritual of the temple could not be more scathing. God is satiated with it, has no delight in it, never required it, hates and regards as a wearisome burden all the solemn assemblies. Long prayers and the ostentatious, ritualistic, spreading out of hands in prayer are as useless an approach to God in the time of Isaiah as of Jesus. We are sometimes told we must treat this condemnation of religious life and practices as exaggeration, because Isaiah received his call vision in the temple, and some scholars confidently assert what festival he was attending there; but it is all assumption. He does not say he was in the temple (6). Just as he had seen contrasted the real Jerusalem and the ideal (1 and 2), so, having condemned the real temple, he had a vision of the true temple in which the Lord was really enthroned surrounded with heavenly beings who proclaimed his glory and holiness, where sins were cleansed, men heard God speaking and, without waiting for a 'call', were inspired to leap forward with a plea to be used in the service of God.

That ideal vision moulded his whole ministry. The holy God to whom Israel was bound had shown his righteousness by all his loyal acts to her in history, and though he had to use Assyria as the rod of his wrath against evil (10.5), yet the purged remnant of Israel would remain. When Jerusalem was surrounded by Assyrian troops, her own mercenaries had deserted and no human aid was possible, Isaiah boldly proclaimed that God would save the city and no arrow would be shot into it (Isa. 37). His faith must have seemed almost as absurd as if a prophet had said the same in Warsaw when Hitler's panzers and dive-bombers had begun their devastating attacks, but history proved him right. As he watched the rapid advance of ruthless Assyrian forces through Palestine he told the people not to panic, for God would cut down the enemy like a lopped branch (10).

He was equally strong in his condemnation of political intrigues and alliances. The threat of a powerful militant nation made him seek, not the armament manufacturers, but God; it sent him not to examine national defences and to plan more powerful nuclear weapons, but to examine the national conscience, make confession to God for the sins which inevitably led to the punishment of war. When temporary victory had been won and people boasted of their successful defences— care of water supplies, fortification of walls—and gave themselves to joy and gladness, slaying oxen and killing sheep, eating flesh and drinking wine, the prophet proclaimed a message as unpopular then as now: Boast not in your own power, give God thanks and confess your sins (22). To Isaiah God was all-powerful, an actual personal force to be reckoned with, not talked about. Surrender to an enemy meant lack of trust in him, entanglement in foreign alliances was disloyalty to the Holy One of Israel. Isaiah sabotaged a projected alliance with Egypt by contrasting Egyptian cavalry with Israel's God, and by the even more dramatic method of walking naked and barefoot through the capital, acting the part of captive Egyptians bound for the prison camps of Assyria (20).

We talk and think as though nations choose war or peace; prophetic faith held that nations and individuals choose sin or goodness, and the inevitable outcome of sin is war sent by a righteous, ruthless, loving God who will not allow men to remain in sin without forcing them to see the meaning of sin through its consequences. The prophets today would ask what is wrong with *our* national aims and policy that there is such international tension and suspicion, and an enormous share of the world's wealth is wasted on armaments. In a lovely contemporaneous poem (2.2-4), quoted too by Micah (4.1-3), we hear the peasants' longing for peace, when swords shall be beaten into ploughshares and spears into pruning hooks.

More than any other prophet, Isaiah regarded drunkenness as the outstanding sin, interfering with a man's religion and making him incapable of fellowship with God. He speaks of drunken men who are heroes in their cups and mighty men of valour in mixing cocktails (5.11ff.), as though wine or strong drink, as they pursued it early in the morning and sat late at night at tables covered with vomit (28.8), gave to their sodden minds a self-confidence that warped their judgment and took away the sense of dependence on God, making them wise in their own eyes and shrewd in their own sight (5.21).

Micah, a contemporary of Isaiah, was the most outspoken critic of religious institutions divorced from social morality. There was communal ownership in land, which at regular intervals was redivided by lot. Micah claimed there was no one who could be trusted to throw the dividing line straight across the fields (2.5). Women were cast out from their pleasant houses and men's livelihood taken away. The prophet called it cannibalism:

'You tear the skin from off my people, and their flesh from off their bones; you eat the flesh of my people, and flay their skin from off them. You break their bones in pieces and chop them up like meat in the pot and like flesh in the cauldron'. (3.3)

His condemnation of princes, priests and prophets, and his prophecy of the coming destruction of Jerusalem (3.12), caused his arrest. He was taken to Jerusalem, tried for his life, and the book of Jeremiah (26.17ff.), over a hundred years later, recalls his famous trial, though he himself does not mention it. He convinced his accusers that he was filled with the power of the spirit of God (Mic. 3.8), and converted even the king, who called the nation to repentance.

Using dramatically the metaphor of a trial scene in his preaching, he pictured God as accusing Israel (6.1ff.). The enduring hills of Palestine that had watched Israel's redemptive history were witnesses, God pleaded all his saving acts; the people convinced of their sin offered to increase to absurd limits their sacrifices:

> *With what shall I come before the Lord,*
> *And bow myself before God on high?*
> *Shall I come before him with burnt offerings,*
> *With calves a year old?*
> *Will the Lord be pleased with thousands of rams*
> *With ten thousands of rivers of oil?*
> *Shall I give my first-born son for my sin,*
> *The fruit of my body for the sin of my soul?* (6.6-7)

And the prophet breaks in with a view of God's requirements which summarise the whole of prophetic belief about the place of conduct in religion:

> *What does the Lord require of you*
> *But acts of justice, an attitude of loving-kindness*
> *and walking humbly with God?* (6.8)

The word translated 'humbly' may mean 'carefully' or, possibly, it carries the picture of a bride walking veiled by her husband, confident, dependent, and committed.

The Babylonian Deluge: Jeremiah, Ezekiel, Second-Isaiah

The three great prophets Jeremiah, Ezekiel, and the anonymous Second-Isaiah knew about the terrible destruction of their temple, nation and homeland, and brought visions of reconstruction. The Babylonian rape of Palestine, the seventy years of exile in a foreign land, and the hope of return, they pictured as God's doings, not international happenings. For all three the important factors were not human policy but God's judgment on man's sin, and the initiative of God's love in forgiveness and restoration.

Brought up in a provincial, priestly home, *Jeremiah* heard God's call, saw God's visions and felt the touch of God's hand when still an unmarried lad. For forty-five years he continued to prophesy, through the first capture of Jerusalem, the eleven years of Babylonian occupation and the final complete destruction of the city; then, choosing to remain in the devastated land (40), for five years he helped to rebuild the national and religious life under a new governor, Gedaliah, at a new capital, Mizpah, and probably in a new religious centre, Bethel. When Gedaliah was murdered by a fellow Jew, the aged prophet was carried off to Egypt by fugitives from Babylonian punitive forces (43) and, according to tradition, was stoned to death there by Jews. No Old Testament figure is known so intimately as this lonely, tragic man. Detailed biography from Baruch, his companion and secretary, and autobiography that lifts the veil into his own thoughts and feelings, both reveal his deep contact with God, his inner struggles, and the anguish of his cross: doing a task to which God called him and held him, remaining among people he loved, sharing their suffering, and foretelling their inevitable doom.

In language comparable to that used in the birth stories of Jesus he heard God saying,

'Before I formed thee in the womb I knew thee, set thee apart before birth, appointed thee a prophet.' (1.5)

Using physical imagery he relates the story, like that of Moses, of the way God called him and overcame his reluctance (1.9). The message came through two common scenes. Through the early almond blossom, by a pun on its Hebrew name, God said he was watchful to fulfil his word (1.11f). A kitchen cauldron boiling over spoke of the suffering God would spill over the land as judgment on evil (1.13f.).

Jeremiah's message was similar to that of other prophets; God had guided through the past, Israel had deserted, 'forsaken me the fountain of living water and hewn out cisterns, cracked cisterns, that can hold no water' (2.13). False priests grabbed at the right to guide; prophets led men away; yet God was pleading with his children, with his people to whom he was bound as by marriage (3.1ff.). Although one good man could have saved the city, corruption was so complete that none could be found (5.1), and the fire of God's word would burn it up, a foreign nation would trample it down. Reform was impossible because 'prophets prophesy falsely, by them the priests rule, and my people love to have it so' (5.31). His famous sermon calling the temple a 'den of robbers' and fore-telling its destruction (7) caused his arrest and trial (26). God, he said, had never ordered their temple ritual: sacrifices, offerings and the burning of children. God's demand was obedience: life together of God and people. Led 'as a gentle lamb to the slaughter' (11.19) by the murderous conspiracy of his relatives, Jeremiah called down God's vengeance on them and fulfilled in too literal a way the later injunction of Jesus (Luke 14.26).

His keen, continual, inner conflict was caused by foreshorten-ing the future and not understanding the patient forbearance of God. He was right about sin and doom, but wrong to see in every invasion God's final act. In the shame of being treated as a false prophet he accused God:

> You have seduced me and I let myself be seduced, you were stronger than I and have prevailed; I am become a laughing stock. (20.7)

When the final blow came he was so sure it was God's doing that he called on the king to surrender, on the army and people to desert and save their own lives lest in fighting against God's agent they should be found fighting God. He narrowly escaped death, saved by a negro slave (38.7ff.).

From Jeremiah's confessions we can learn much about the mechanics of inspiration and the way God spoke to men. His-tory showed that words of peace and comfort to the impenitent, especially if given by a paid professional, were always suspect. False prophets were those who stubbornly insisted on their own visions and dreams rather than seeking God's words, those who stole others' sermons, and those whose private lives were immoral (14; 23; 29.23). But for Jeremiah the ultimate test was a value judgment, 'if you utter the precious and not the worth-less you shall be my mouthpiece' (Jer. 15.19). The judgment was not always easy to make; in his public debate with Hana-niah he had to wait for God's answer (28), and on another occasion it was ten days before he could give God's message to panic-stricken enquirers—and then it was too late (42.7).

But in the preaching of even Jeremiah there was hope. The divine potter patiently worked until from the most intractable clay he had moulded the best possible vessel (18); although Israel had broken his covenant, he would take the initiative, forgive and forget their sins, win their consent to a new covenant written on their hearts and give all of them intimate friendship with himself (31.31ff.); houses and fields would once again be bought and sold in devastated Palestine (32).

It is probable that *Ezekiel* was a contemporary of Jeremiah, and both may have prophesied in Jerusalem, but the story of Ezekiel has been confused—possibly by combining a biography with an autobiography (see the first two verses of the book). He was probably descended from the priests at Jerusalem, and his theology has many more links with priests than with prophets. His call-vision shows the attempt to break away from human images to describe God, he heaps up abstract words as in the phrase, 'the likeness of the appearance of a man' (1.26); but for him as for Jesus at his call 'the heavens were opened' (1.1). For him, as for Jeremiah, taste was used as a metaphor as well as touch, sight and hearing (3.2; cf. Jer. 15, 16). But it is difficult to translate his experiences into literal modern terms. The main call-vision reconciled Isaiah's belief that because God dwelt there Jerusalem was safe, with Jeremiah's prophecy of destruction. A flying platform, constructed so that it could take off in any direction without turning, carried God from the temple before its destruction to accompany his people into exile (11.22f.). After the exile it led them back, and God re-entered the rebuilt temple through the east end, which had ever to remain closed (43.4; 44.2).

To Ezekiel the destruction was the working-out of the wrath or fury of God against evil, which must be unsparingly and pitilessly smitten for the sake of God's nature or name. Because God is holy, sin and its adherents must be wiped out; but punishment is saving, it springs from the fact that God remembers his covenant. He acts first, brings a sense of shame to sinners and forgives them (16.61; 36), breaking the entail of the past. Ezekiel (18) finding the exiles in despair, suffering for the sins of previous generations, preached a doctrine that ignored habit, character and social science. God has no delight in the death of a sinner and looks for the first glimmer of change. If a bad man repents he is saved, if a good man sins he is damned whatever the record of the past. Always in the rapidly passing present every man has the power to break with the past and change the direction of life. There is truth in Ezekiel's teaching; we blame ourselves for failure because we know we could have chosen, acted, differently. The Bible faith is that God is interested in individuals as well as groups, and a new Israel can be born from new Israelites. But Israelites cannot make themselves new. God creates new hearts (36.26), he restores and forgives, and that leads men to repentance and new life (20.42 ff.). Continually it is stressed that the initiative always lies with God.

The sins on Ezekiel's list are difficult to classify; largely they spring from his priestly background, where blood was holy, taboo, belonging to God. Ritual crimes, acts of indecency, moral and ethical sins jostle each other in his condemnations; but all of them are really acts of disobedience to the will of God made known in law, social life and conscience (18; 22); they are acts against the known nature of God.

More than any of the prophets, Ezekiel looks over his shoulder into the future. In picturesque language as full of vivid imagery as the story of his call and the account of Israel's sinful past (16), he paints what is to be. God will act first— not in love for Israel, nor for the sake of Israel, but in pity for his holy name profaned, to sanctify his great name. As in Psalm 23, his 'name's sake' provides the surest basis for confidence and hope, for nothing can change God's name and nature. Israel will be restored; the dead dry bones will become an exceeding great army when God's breath, the wind, is blown into them (37); the old divisions between north and south will disappear from the reunited Israel; a last great battle against evil forces will be decisively won by the power of God (39).

The final nine chapters of the book of Ezekiel contain a vision of a completely reconstructed land, a new capital with a new temple as the centre of it all. The country will be redivided among the twelve tribes, whose land will lie to north and south of the city. On east and west will lie the domain of the civil ruler, a prince not a king. In the centre the land of the priests will surround the sanctuary, insulating the holiness of the central shrine where God will dwell. The new name of the city will be 'The Lord is There'.

It appears from his book that Jeremiah, facing the destruction of city and temple because of Israel's sins and religious abuses, had envisaged a religion without a temple or its ritual, comparable to the vision Jesus pictured for his Samaritan questioner (John 4). Ezekiel, however, believed that a purged temple and a purged cultus was necessary to embody and give form to the religion of the purged community. Priests had failed to make clear the distinction between the holy and the secular, clean and unclean, sabbath and weekday (22.26). Although he believed that all life belonged to God, yet it was necessary to attach special holiness to certain persons, places, days and things, in order that this protected holiness could spread throughout the whole, removing uncleanness, and hallowing all.

Three other prophets of the exilic period who helped to rebuild nation, religion and national home also stressed the importance of the temple. *Haggai* and *Zechariah* led in the rebuilding of the temple, and spoke of the temple as the condition of God's blessing. *Malachi*—the word meaning 'my messenger' used for another anonymous prophet—drew a picture of the windows of heaven as opening outwards, but being blocked up by the heaps of unpaid tithes due from the people. God could not open the windows and pour out his blessing till the unpaid tithes had been paid into the storehouse (3.10).

The danger of Ezekiel's stress in Judaism, as in all religion, is that the material aids to worship and fellowship with God become ends in themselves. God is shut away from men in buildings guarded by numerous intermediaries, and religion, far from sanctifying all life, becomes a separate part of life, practised on a special day in special clothes.

We do not know who wrote *Isaiah* 40-66. Much may be the work of a man who was also called Isaiah; or of someone who chose the name because of his sympathy with his great predecessor Isaiah of Jerusalem; or who deliberately remained anonymous because he had no wish to be roasted alive—the fate Babylonians imposed on nationalist prophets (Jer. 29.22). We do not know how much of these chapters is by one man, at one time or place, nor where that place was. But the book of Second-Isaiah—to use the name by which he is generally known—is the high-water mark of Old Testament religion. His call came through a voice proclaiming that amid all that is transitory God's word, his promise and revelation, alone is enduring.

> Hark! someone saying 'Cry out'; and I said, 'What shall I cry out?' 'All flesh is grass and all its graciousness like a wild flower. Grass withers, a flower fades, but the word of our God endures for ever.' (40.6f.)

A second voice proclaimed the triumphant return of God at the head of his forgiven and restored people, an act that would reveal to all the glory of the Lord. It is a message of comfort and gladness comparable to the joy of the Easter morning. Evangelists are called out to proclaim the glorious news that God is coming. 'Behold your God' rings out in complete contrast to the doom with which Amos threatened men when God should appear. We have looked at the prophet's picture of the incomparable majesty of God seen in creation, and his amazing tenderness in his care for his children, bringing them home again, removing their despondency and giving them a new kind of strength. But God's greatness was also seen in history. On the horizon a deliverer, Cyrus the Persian, has appeared whom 'victory attends at every step' (41.2). He is God's friend, his shepherd, even his anointed Messiah for whom the nation

had been longing and whom the prophets had foretold (45.1);
he will rebuild the waste places and set God's people free.
God has called him and girded him. If we ask what right the
historians and prophets of Israel had to say they discerned
God in history, Second-Isaiah's answer is that God fulfilled
the promises he had made through the prophets of old; the
prophet himself had been interpreting contemporary events in
terms of God's purpose and character, and every day new
events were proving correct the outcome he had predicted from
the pattern of God's actions in the past. Dramatically he
challenged the heathen to prove the existence of their gods by
the same evidence. Israel's Lord alone is God, known from
what he *does*, but great and glorious beyond the power of man
to portray what he *is*.

The prophet never tired of talking of the Servant of the
Lord, and four poems are sometimes separated as a unity
relating the story of the servant (42.1-4; 49.1-6; 50.4-9; 52.
13-53, 12). In some ways the portrait reminds us of Jeremiah,
but it is composite and clearly some features interpret aspects of
Israel's history and predict God's purpose for her in the future.
Under the figure of a great leader rejected, suffering, and
finally slain by the sins of others, Second-Isaiah depicted the
history of the nation; but death was not the end. God intervened, took and vindicated his righteous servant, and from the
amazed nations, watching the drama of sacrifice, death and resurrection, many were saved and healed by the strokes that
had fallen on the righteous one, revealing the meaning of their
sin. Humble and unobtrusive, the servant carries the knowledge
of God to the Gentile world, patiently encouraging the slightest
response till the full light of the truth blazes forth. Like a lamb
slain at the altar, in his death he bears the sins of those who
slay him. He is the light of the world, the covenant binding
the world to God. The picture changed the old idea of a national
God bound to his chosen people, and substituted the idea of a
people chosen to serve and die for the world and to share their
greatest national possession—their God—with the world.

The prophecy, still unfulfilled, was used by New Testament

writers to interpret the meaning of the life, death and resurrection of Jesus who died for many, bare our sins in his own body, and by whose stripes we are healed. With Second-Isaiah, grace became a personal relationship in which God takes the initiative, patiently seeks to fan to a flame the dimmest insight into his purposes, and encourages the slightest, most faltering response. Suffering also gained a new meaning and purpose; its intercession could bring peace, healing and acceptance by God. The vision of the writer of the book of Jonah had been carried a stage further. Not only must Jews carry the message of a merciful, loving God to those who despitefully use them, but they must be willing to lose their own life that the world may be saved. It is a vision that no branch of the New Israel—the Christian Church—has yet seen for itself.

4

GOD'S KINSHIP WITH MAN

THE CLAIM made in Old Testament theology is that the great
God who acts in creation and in history, who speaks to and
through prophets words of moral condemnation, comfort and
hope, can be called Father. He is loving and responsive, and
interested in the details of our daily life. He is the God not only
of the world and nature, of history and nations, but of the
individual. Jesus taught,

> 'Take no anxious thought, saying What shall we eat, or what shall
> we drink, or what shall we wear? For the Gentiles seek all these
> things; and your heavenly Father knows that you need them
> all' (Matt. 6.31);

and he told some stories that pictured God seeking one man as
a shepherd seeks one lost sheep, and rejoicing over one sinner
that repents (Luke 15). There is the same vivid contrast between
God the great creator and God the Father in the two parallel
stories of creation in Genesis. In the first the majestic God
utters his voice and the whole universe is created, men and
women spring into existence; and in the second, the Gardener
plants his garden, moulds one by one man and beast from clay,
builds a woman round a rib taken from sleeping man. Second-
Isaiah made the same contrast; it is the same one God who
gently leads his flock and sustains the heavenly hosts (40.11, 26).
Old Testament writers held firmly to the belief that the greatness of God was unsearchable and his knowledge too wonderful for man; but they were equally certain that the word that
revealed God

> 'is not too hard for you, neither is it far off. It is not in heaven
> that you should say, Who will go up for us to heaven and bring

it to us and make us hear it that we may do it? . . . The word is very near you, it is in your mouth and in your heart so that you can do it' (Deut. 30.11f.).

Old Testament theology thinks of God not only in terms of what he *does* in deed and word, believing that he unveils himself to man in action; but it believes that he reveals what he *is*, his being, in his relationship with men, his availability to men, his influence on men's attitude to life's problems. The Old Testament is absolutely certain that man cannot separate himself from God.

The Group and God's Righteousness

Offence is often caused by the statement that God visits the sins of the fathers on the children to the third and fourth generation (Deut. 5.9). It is contrasted with the law 'Fathers shall not be put to death for their children, nor shall the children be put to death for the fathers; every man shall be put to death for his own sin' (Deut. 24.16), and with the prophetic dictum, that the son shall not suffer for the sin of the father nor the father for the son (Ezek. 18.20).

The first statement reflects the social theory called either 'corporate personality' or 'defective individuality', which holds that both in society and in the sight of God man is treated as part of the larger group of which he is a member. Within the family, clan or tribe each member has the same flesh and through his veins runs the common blood and, as we do not think of any limb as separate from the body as a whole, so no individual is thought of as separate from the one body of the group; an injury to one member sheds the common blood. Among the Semites the kinship of blood produced a very closely-knit society, maintained by common meals, blood rites and sacrifices. The head of the group was regarded as, in a sense, the representative of the whole group, and his actions committed the family of which he was head. When Achan stole the wedge of gold the social unit of which he was head was put to death because his sin had brought guilt on all (Josh. 7).

This Old Testament thought recurs in the New Testament, where Paul uses the same corporate idea to explain the meaning of the death of Jesus. Adam was the first man and head of the human race; his sin committed all men because all were part of his group; and in his sentence of death for sin all were involved (I Cor. 15.22). God made a new beginning for the human race in Jesus, a new head; members of his group are free from the heritage of Adam's sin and death, sharing the victory over sin and death won by Jesus, his achievement in complete obedience to the will of God. We pass from the wrath of God into his love, forgiven and accepted by God because of our union in his corporate body—to be a Christian, to join the Church, puts a man 'in Christ'.[1]

Similarly the Old Testament could think of God as part of the group, and a man's obligations to his group included obligations to the God of the group. Like man God too had his 'righteousness', or the loyalty that was required of him. We have seen that 'righteousness' cuts right across our narrow ideas of justice. In the Old Testament, judgment is not simply punishing the wicked, but coming to the rescue of the needy:

> *Give justice to the weak and the fatherless;*
> *Maintain the rights of the afflicted and the destitute.*
> *Rescue the weak and the needy,*
> *Deliver them from the hand of the wicked* (Ps. 82.3f.)

In justice there was more mercy than we recognise, and in righteousness, justice and mercy were not opposed terms. So strong was this element of mercy or benevolence in 'righteousness' that in later Hebrew the word becomes the usual term for almsgiving (cf. Matt. 6.1f.)—that is, for gifts to needy members of the group, which cannot legally be demanded, but are an obligation. Righteousness was within man's power to attain, and without it there was woe and social wrong (Jer. 22.3,13). The Psalmist thinks of man as possessing this divine quality, speaking of the 'God of my righteousness' (4.1) and

[1] J. V. Taylor, *The Primal Vision*, shows that there are still African tribes who think of man in this corporate way.

pleading that God will judge him according to his righteousness and integrity (7.8). It is the ground on which man is confident he will see God, and the reason he claims reward. There are good descriptions of the righteous (Ps. 37; 92); and the righteous of Psalm 37.29 becomes, in the teaching of Jesus, the meek who will inherit the earth (Matt. 5.5). Between the righteous and God there is a special relationship; he delivers them when they cry, is their refuge and sustains them so that they are never moved; he loves them and they are glad and trust him. One Psalmist uses a metaphor similar to Paul's when he says that the righteous enter the house of God's righteous acts from which the wicked are shut out, and that their names are written in the book of those who live (69.27). It seems probable that in the New Testament when the word was used by both Jesus and Paul it carried a broader meaning than legal justice, including loyalty to family relationship and needs.

God too has his righteousness (Ex. 9.27; Deut. 32.4), and nearly always when God's 'righteousnesses' are mentioned the reference is to his loyal acts. At the wells, women recounted God's righteous acts in delivering Israel (Judg. 5.11). Samuel's farewell address reviewed the past national history under the title 'The righteous acts of the Lord' (I Sam. 12.7). Isaiah revolutionised the idea of God's holiness by declaring that it was revealed by his historical acts (5.16), proving that he fulfilled his obligations to the nation to which he was linked. When he saved men he gave them, as a blessing, righteousness together with loving-kindness and faithfulness. It was the subject of men's preaching and, like Paul who determined to know nothing but Jesus Christ and him crucified (I Cor. 2.2), so the Psalmist declared he would talk of nothing but the righteous acts of God (71.16). It is Isaiah 40-66 that speaks most often of God's righteousness. Facing great opposition because he claimed that Cyrus, the heathen conqueror, was the Messiah or the Christ, the prophet stated that God had called Cyrus in righteousness—in full accord with his loyalty to Israel (42.2). Often the word can be translated there as victory (45.12). God's righteous acts bring success and, as the Hebrew thought in terms of consequences not causes, righteousness, deliverance, salvation, and victory were synonymous words.

God's righteousness is also especially linked with the glories of the hoped-for golden age or messianic kingdom. It will be upheld by judgment and loyal acts (Isa. 9.7); the messianic ruler will judge by it and wear it as a garment (11.4). It will bring peace, quietness and security (32.15ff.), and is one of the foundations of God's throne (Ps. 89.14). But the Bible knows nothing of a universe that includes heaven and not hell; nor of a theology of a loving God who does not destroy evil. The puritan preacher who talked of taking men by the seat of their trousers and shaking them over hell-fire, and thought of the joys of the saved being increased by the sight of the damned, could find ground for his beliefs, 'The righteous will rejoice when he sees the vengeance' (Ps. 58.10). The wonderful book of Isaiah 40-66 ends with a similar picture:

> For as the new heaven and the new earth, which I shall make, shall remain before me, says the Lord, so shall your descendants and your name remain. From new moon to new moon and from sabbath to sabbath, all flesh shall come to worship before me, says the Lord. And they shall go forth and look on the dead bodies of the men that have rebelled against me: for their worm shall not die, their fire shall not be quenched: and they shall be an abhorring to all flesh.

Perhaps the fact that Jesus quoted from this passage suggests that the truth in the words passed over into Christianity, and cannot be conveniently discarded as a superseded idea from the Old Testament (Mark 9.48). Yet the God who ruthlessly destroys evil and the malignant evildoer shows his righteousness by forgiving the sinner. He confers on man righteousness, the right standing in the community (Isa. 50.8). The new name for the Messiah will be 'God is our righteousness' (Jer. 23.6), a title comparable with 'Christ is our peace' (Eph. 2.14). Though in Exodus (23.7) it is stated that God does not declare the wicked to be righteous, yet in bold contradiction Paul claims that now God does just this. As the righteousness of ten men could have saved Sodom, and the suffering and death of the righteous servant could put into a position of having been loyal to their obligations many who clearly did not deserve it, so 'in Christ' we can be restored to the fellowship of God. With Second-Isaiah (45.24) we can exclaim, 'In the Lord I have righteousness and strength', or with Bunyan we can cry of the Christ, 'There is my righteousness'.

God and the Individual

'The savage emphasised the tribe and had social relationships; the Greek discovered the individual and we have to put up with the consequences.' The secular and religious world is still torn between the rival ideas of the Greek and the savage. One view stresses the importance of the state, Church, community: the individual is subordinate to the community and has his worth as part of the larger whole. The other view places the emphasis on the individual for which the community is thought to exist: the purpose of life is the creation of free, responsible, developing persons.

Jeremiah was conscious of an intense personal relationship with God, and was forced to act as a God-controlled individual against the group; but he taught that the new covenant written on the hearts of individuals was made with the house of Israel. The community will be saved by changed individuals within it. Jesus was in line with this prophetic teaching when he brought together the world and the individual: God so loved the world that he sent his son into the world that the world through him might be saved; and the method was that whosoever believes in him shall be saved (John 3.16). Even in primitive society disputes between individuals were adjudicated, and an individual could be punished by being 'cut off from his people'; but the group suffered with the sinner.

Jeremiah and Ezekiel heard dispirited survivors of the Babylonian destruction using a proverb, 'The fathers have eaten sour grapes and the children's teeth are set on edge' (Ezek. 18.2; Jer. 31.29)—our fathers sinned and we are bound by the consequences, the past is irrevocable and we are its helpless slaves. God's word to Ezekiel met that situation. It denied the truth of the second commandment. God does not punish children to the third or fourth generation for their fathers' sins; each person will be punished for his own sins. In revolt against accepted belief, the 'word' went right over to the other extreme: not only does a man not suffer for his father's sins but he does not suffer for his own sins if he changes, and conversely the good man gets no credit for his goodness if he sins. Ezekiel's message as we have seen, ignores the cumulative effect of past sin on society, the growth of individual character, and puts the emphasis, where Jesus put it, on the will of the individual. Whatever truth there may be in corporate personality or determinism, there are no chains from the past which cannot be broken. But we must not read into Ezekiel's message any modern ideas about the rights or value of the individual; the stress was on the responsibility of the individual, and like Jeremiah, Ezekiel appealed to the 'house of Israel' (18.25-32). Both prophets aimed at safeguarding the community from disasters due to the sins of individuals, and at rebuilding the new people.

The Old Testament prophetic theology was that God loved and chose Israel. When she rebelled he sent chosen individuals to recall her to himself. The basis of his choice was changed, by being restricted first to responsive Israelites; finally it included at least some Gentiles (Deut. 23.8). Jesus in his talk to Nicodemus (John 3) claimed that even the restricted Israelite limitation had finally gone: God loved the world and accepted anyone who responded. The mode of God's choice appeared as arbitrary in the first century AD as in the seventeenth BC. To use Paul's phrase it was 'of grace' (Rom. 11.5), resulting from God's freewill. Man's faith or response was his only qualification, and God's purpose was to save the world. 'By grace are you saved through faith, and that, not of yourselves, it is the gift of God' (Eph. 2.8).

God as Parent

The land of Palestine when Israel entered it, and the Canaanites among whom she settled, had a religion that was largely

D

bound up with nature and the recurring seasons, with ritual to obtain and retain fertility of the soil, the flocks and human beings. Some of this ritual, and much of its language and thought, Israel took over from her neighbours, but most of it was either condemned or transformed by the prophets. It is doubtful whether Israel ever accepted from Canaanite religion the belief that God was the ancestor of the tribe or begat men, but it is clear that he was thought of as concerned in every act of human conception and was called Father. Eve, punning on the name of Cain, said that with God she had gotten a child (Gen. 4.1). Outstanding leaders, as well as Israel herself, are spoken of as formed by God in the womb; and the Psalmist sings:

> *Thou didst form my inward parts,*
> *Thou didst knit me together in my mother's womb.* (Ps. 139)

God is also represented as promising to be a father to Solomon (II Sam. 7.14) and in Psalm 2, which appears to be part of a coronation service, God says to the new crowned king, 'You are my son, today have I begotten you.' Usually it is the people who are represented as his sons. Jeremiah says that Ephraim is God's firstborn (31.9), and Hosea likens God to a father teaching his child to walk and calling Israel, his son, out of Egypt (11.3). Isaiah speaks of God as nourishing and bringing up children, and continually in the Psalter the same metaphor is used: when earthly father and mother forsake me the Lord will look after me (Ps. 27.10); God is the father of the fatherless and sets the solitary in families (68.6); he is addressed as 'My father, my God' (89.26); and we are told that as a father pities his children so the Lord pities those who worship him (103.13). Jeremiah (2.27) relates that in his day people worshipped in front of wood and stone and said to a wooden post, 'You are my father', and to a stone pillar, 'You gave me birth'; but one prophet shows that for him at least this was a metaphor,

Yet O Lord thou art our father; we are the clay and thou art the potter, we are all the work of thy hand. (Isa. 64.8)

It is probable that we must interpret in the same way personal names like Abi*jah* and Ahi*jah*, which link the name of Israel's God with 'father' and 'brother'.

The Old Testament idea of the fatherhood of God seems to arise firstly from the concept of the creator who formed man, understood him and had compassion; he set men in families and expected them to be faithful to each other as members of a family that called him Father (Mal. 2.10). There was an affection and kinship that was sometimes clouded by the wrath of God, but this always gave way to the permanent relationship of love (Ps. 30.5); and with this thought there was a danger that people would abuse their kinship, believing that whatever they did God would not, could not, cease to be bound to them. The second concept in 'Fatherhood' was that of ruler or master of children; God educated and disciplined his children even through affliction (Deut. 8.5); they owed him obedience but rebelled and questioned his rights. In later Judaism the 'Father in Heaven' has more of this meaning of kingship and ruler, and the emphasis is on power rather more than love. There is an often-quoted saying of the Jewish fathers, perhaps contemporaneous with Jesus, 'Be strong as a leopard, swift as an eagle, fleet as a gazelle, brave as a lion to do the will of thy father which is in heaven'. In the New Testament, terms drawn from primitive ideas of physical descent from God, and from poetic imagery that regarded God as specially concerned in the conception of those who became outstanding leaders, are used to explain the consciousness of a unique relationship between himself and God which Jesus clearly had, although it must be remembered that his kinship with David is traced through an earthly father and in the words of Jesus himself there is no hint whatever of the old physical sonship. Yet once (John 5.17) he seems to have used 'my father' in a way that gave Jewish hearers the impression that he claimed a special relationship that made him equal with God; and like the king at his coronation Jesus heard a voice addressing him as 'Son' at his 'call' when he committed himself publicly to the kingdom at Baptism.

The Old Testament also includes in the idea of the parent-hood of God the thought of the mother-child relationship:

Can a woman forget her suckling child
that she should have no compassion on the son of her womb?
Even these may forget,
Yet I will not forget you. (Isa. 49.15)

The relationship is even closer in the Hebrew, for the word usually translated 'to have compassion' links with the word for 'womb' and seems to denote the special relationship between mother and child; it is often used of the Lord's attitude to his people. The Moabite Stone, relating the destruction in the eighth century BC of the Israelite sanctuary on Mount Nebo, uses the word 'wombs' for the many female slaves—probably sacred prostitutes—maintained at the temple there. Progress in religion comes through new interpretation of old ideas, rediscovery of essential truths however deeply buried, and ruthless jettisoning of unessential accidentals though ancient and beloved, and the prophets of Israel were fearless in using and transmuting forms and ideas from heathen religion. Perhaps they took this word, which would suggest 'wombs' to their hearers, to emphasise the tender, motherly character of God and the completeness of his parenthood.

God as Husband

In early seasonal religion, the nature God was thought of as the husband of the land. The word used was Baal, a word that denotes 'one who possesses certain rights over someone or something'. Joseph was a '*baal* of dreams' (Gen. 37.19). It was the usual word for a human husband, being used as late as Jeremiah (31.32) of God's relations with Israel. It is quite clear that Israel used the word as a divine name for her own God, but Hosea (2.16), realising the great dangers of syncretism between Canaanite and Hebrew religion arising from it, forbade the use of the word at all in Israel even by a woman for her own husband; he must in future be called 'my man' not 'my baal'. But Hosea was also the prophet who, from his own bitter experience of an unsuccessful marriage, used the metaphor of the husband to describe God's relationship with Israel. Amos (3.2) had used 'know', a word expressing the intimacy of married life; Hosea (2) spoke of God as having loved and married Israel, but she forsook him and became mistress of others from whom she thought she could get more material gains. Jeremiah (3) used the same picture of God as married to two sisters, Judah and Israel, both of whom deserted him; and Ezekiel (16) spoke of Israel as a baby girl abandoned at birth, found and cared for by God, who married her and to whom she owed everything.

The central value of this symbolism seems to have been that the prophets made the people realise that their link with God was conditional on obedience to his will, faithful loyalty to him alone. Although marriage, like the parent bond, involved the tie of kinship—Adam greeted his wife as 'flesh of my flesh and bone of my bones, (Gen. 2.23)—yet the bond was not indissoluble: divorce was possible. We have seen that Hosea did not contemplate divorce between God and Israel, any more than between himself and his faithless wife; God would buy Israel back, take away the material possessions that had snared her away and win her again (2f.). Jeremiah went even further and pictured God as doing the strange, scandalous thing of taking back a divorced wife (3.1); and Second-Isaiah denied that God ever made out a bill of divorce (50. 1). But Ezekiel, describing their desertion and adultery with crude, lewd details pronounced that both Israel and Judah should die the death of harlots and adulterous women (23.47). The prophets did not really believe God would ever completely and finally break with Israel, or allow her to be destroyed. There would be a remnant however small and insignificant, like the shoots from the stump of a felled tree (Isa. 6.13). A new covenant binding God and Israel together was preached by both Jeremiah (31.31) and Ezekiel (34.25).

Second-Isaiah broke from the idea of Israel as a 'peculiar people' and substituted a 'covenant people' (42.6; 49.8) who would be God's servant and his witness to the nations. But this writer returned to a description of God which reasserted the older kinship idea rather than that of the covenant. He never tired of calling God the 'redeemer' of Israel (41.14 and twelve times). The Hebrew word thus translated here and in Job (19.25) meant 'next-of-kin'. It was the next-of-kin's duty to buy back less fortunate relatives who had been sold for debt or who were slaves; but his duties were also wider. The story of Ruth and Boaz shows a next-of-kin fulfilling his duties even at peril to his own heritage. The laws of blood revenge laid on the next-of-kin the duty of avenging the death of a kinsman; the next-of-kin was bound by unbreakable ties to help, rescue and vindicate. In a bold figure of speech which has greatly influenced Christian phraseology, Second-Isaiah applies the term to God, who is about to rescue Israel from Exile and restore her to her land.

When 'redeemer' is used to translate the word 'next-of-kin' in the Old Testament, the English nuance of 'buying back' or paying a ransom price should not be read into the word. It is a metaphor drawn from the family circle, rather than from the law-courts. The close link is with kinship, and with all the wonderful words used in the Old Testament to describe God's loyal acts, his loving-kindness, his concern for his children, and his saving and rescuing them from slavery and sin.

5

THE GLORY OF GOD

WHEN ALL has been done to attempt to express God's self-revealing nature and his nearness and kinship with man, no introduction to Old Testament theology would be complete without the recognition that throughout the whole book God is different from man. There is a glory, a beauty of holiness, an 'otherness' about him that defies description and makes the language of deeds, words and relationships totally inadequate.

God's Dwelling Place

The Hebrew word translated 'glory' can be used of human splendour. Joseph told his brothers to report all his 'splendour' to his father when they returned to Palestine (Gen. 45.13). The priestly robes have a 'glorious' beauty (Ex. 28.2). When the word is used of God, it is thought of as a great light or devouring fire. If we think of the holiness of God as the potential in a high tension cable, then the glory is the flash that shows that contact has been made or that the power is switched on. When God was present in the tabernacle, the tent of meeting or the temple, his presence was pictured as a bright light so intense and brilliant that neither Moses nor priests could enter (Ex. 40.34: II Chron. 5.14). On the mountain where the law was given, the imagery was rather of the thunder cloud through which the dangerous lightning flash was seen, striking and burning all that was not holy (Ex. 24.16f.) Again, as with the language of the prophets, we do not know whether those who wrote the stories were using the language as conscious symbols; but the priestly experience expressed in the language is clearly akin to the vision spoken of in the hymn of Thomas Binney:

> *Eternal light, Eternal light,*
> *How pure the soul must be,*
> *When placed within thy searching sight,*
> *It shrinks not, but with calm delight,*
> *Can live, and look on thee.*

Ideally God's glory will fill the whole earth, but even this glory is not independent of man. Though the heavens declare it (Ps.19), man must make it known too (Ps. 96), and God requires from man the recognition of his glory as men praise him in corporate worship.

That God was available to men was a corollary of the belief that he revealed himself. In the story of the Garden of Eden the fellowship between God and man is expressed in the statement that the sound of God walking in the garden could be heard when the cool breeze of evening blew (Gen. 3.8). It was sin that broke the intimacy, shutting man out from God's presence; and much nearer the other end of the Old Testament period Second-Isaiah spoke as though there were still barriers between God and men that meant that God was not always available: 'Seek the Lord while he lets himself be found, call upon him while he is near' (Isa. 55.6).

In the patriarchal stories, and as late as the choice of Jerusalem as the site for the Temple, shrines were places where God had in a special way made himself known, and shown his glory. The writers had no difficulty in believing God could appear in human, recognisable form, although as we have seen, we must remember that the word translated 'angel' means also 'messenger' and that there is not *necessarily* any implication of a supernatural figure. That the writers were not trying to give a scientific account is clear from the confusion in most of the stories: often the 'messenger of the Lord' became the Lord himself who disappeared as mysteriously as he appeared (cf. Ex. 3.2f.).

In early Israelite traditions, retained in the national poetry, God was regarded as dwelling in a mountain in the Edomite desert south of Palestine, variously called Sinai, Horeb or Paran. There he met Moses and thither Elijah fled to regain

Moses' experience of direct contact with God (I Kings 19). Thence also, in the hymns sung in worship, he was pictured as riding on the wings of the wind, or the thunder storm, or the cherub that symbolised the spirit of the wind, to succour his people in their need. The song of Deborah spoke of him as going forth from Seir, and marching out from the land of Edom (Judg. 5). The poem called the 'song of Moses' said:

> The Lord came from Sinai, and dawned from Seir upon us;
> He shone forth from Mount Paran, he came from the ten thousands
> of holy ones. (Deut. 33.2)

Another psalmist used the same imagery:

> God came from Teman, and the Holy One from Mount Paran.
> (Hab. 3. 3)

There was a tradition that when they wandered through the wilderness and moved into the land where they settled, the Israelites had portable shrines that symbolised—or actually were, we cannot be sure—the real presence of God. There was the 'tent of meeting' or the tabernacle (Ex. 25f; 33), over which the light of the glory of God showed his presence or availability. But supremely it was the wooden box or ark overlaid with gold that assured God's presence, and the lid of the ark overshadowed by the winged forms of cherubs was the empty throne symbolising the presence of the unseen God. There is a story that there had been another God-given symbol that Israel had worshipped, but it had led her astray and was rejected and destroyed. When Moses was absent, Aaron had put gold into a furnace and a golden bull image had come out and was greeted with the cry 'This is your God, O Israel, that brought you out of the land of Egypt' (Ex. 32). A similar image was used in the northern kingdom at the time of the division of the nation into two parts, and was greeted with the same cry, it too being another empty throne of the unseen God (I Kings 12.28) But the bull image, symbolising power and fertility, was probably linked with Canaanite worship and was certainly likely to bring a more dangerous concept into religion than the symbol of the invisible wind, and it is understandable why it was rejected.

There was a processional hymn used when the ark was moved by the wandering Israelites:

> And when ever the ark set out Moses said, 'Arise, O Lord, and let thy enemies be scattered; and let them that hate thee flee before thee.' And when it rested, he said, 'Return, O Lord, to the ten thousand thousands of Israel' (Num. 10.35f.).

Possibly a similar ritual was observed at Temple festivals in Jerusalem, when the gates of the temple were bidden to lift up their heads that the King of Glory might enter (Ps. 24). When the ark was carried into battle against the Philistines they cried 'God has come into the camp', and when the ark was captured the priest cried 'The Glory has departed' (I Sam. 4). The same imagery, speaking of the empty space on the ark's lid as the throne of God, is seen in Jeremiah's statement that after the Babylonian exile men would forget about the ark, and Jerusalem itself would be thought of as God's throne (Jer. 3.17). The idea of the ark offered a form of imageless worship before the throne of the invisible God.

From this thought of the movable ark, God was pictured as transferring his residence with his people to Palestine. David, driven out by the jealousy of Saul, said he was told 'Go, serve other gods' (I Sam. 26.19). Naaman, cleansed of his leprosy, asked for two mules' load of earth that in Assyria he might worship Israel's God on Israel's soil (II Kings 5.17). After the temple had been built in Jerusalem, men pictured it as God's dwelling, where he was available. Isaiah spoke of the Lord who dwells on Mount Zion. Amos (1.2) and Joel (3.16) used the same poem:

> *The Lord roars from Zion*
> *and utters his voice from Jerusalem.*

Much later Ezra spoke of God as the one who is in Jerusalem (Ezra 1.3). Men went to Jerusalem to worship him or to 'see his face'. Jeremiah (7.12) and the Deuteronomic writers (Deut.

12.11) used a more ambiguous, metaphorical term speaking of 'the place where God causes his name to dwell', perhaps with stress not on the actual presence but on the place where men could gain contact with the nature or essence of God.

When the temple was about to be, or had been, destroyed, Ezekiel in his visions returned to the idea of a moving God, who went with his people, leaving his temple dwelling-place on the cherub-borne throne accompanying his exiles, and returning with them when they came back to the new Jerusalem.

After the return from exile, it appears that rival claims for the location of the new temple caused another writer to proclaim that no earthly building was good enough for God's dwelling:

> Heaven is my throne, and the earth my footstool.
> What is the house which you would build for me? (Isa. 66)

The writer of the prayer of Solomon at the dedication of the first temple uses similar words:

> But will God indeed dwell on the earth?
> Behold heaven and the highest heaven cannot contain thee,
> How much less this house which I have built. (I Kings 8.27)

In his conversation with the Samaritan woman Jesus is reported to have said that neither in Jerusalem nor on Mount Gerizim will God be worshipped, but true worshippers will worship him in spirit and truth (John 4.21). Jesus, like Jeremiah, appears to have prophesied the destruction of the temple, and it was the only accusation against him on which witnesses agreed at his trial. God is no longer thought of as localised in any building made with man's hands, but in men and women who love him and keep his word (John 14.23; Acts 17.24f.); it is human beings, not buildings, who are the temple of the living God (II Cor. 6). Religious buildings have obviously a high value for corporate worship. They can be places where prayer is wont to be made, trysting places where men meet with God; but they can be a liability to religion. They can symbolise the removal of God from ordinary life, widening the gulf between common life and organised religion, stabilising religion so that it becomes formal and ceases to be a missionary force. There was in Judaism—as there is in Christianity—a tension between home and church, between the church-in-the-home and the church-in-a-holy-building. In Judaism this tension was seen in the struggle as to whether the central festival of Passover was a family festival to be celebrated at home, or a national one when men gathered at the temple (Ex. 12; Deut. 16); but in at least one Hebrew tradition the centre for religious instruction was the home, and the responsibility for it lay on the head of the family (Deut. 6.20ff.). In both Judaism and Christianity, buildings and the vested interests that grew up around them provided a powerful incentive to disunity, both among the different forms of the religion and, more important, between man and God. The whole knowable universe—the heaven of heavens—should be the holy place where we meet God. As Paul suggests, all days are holy days; no place, time or task should be free from the sacredness of his presence. The real crime of the priests in the time of Ezekiel was not that 'they made no distinction between the holy and the common, neither have they taught men the difference between the unclean and the clean' (22.26). It was that they allowed any part of life to be common or unclean (Acts 10.15).

Man's Attitude to Life

We have seen that the glory of God is thought of as not independent of man. Man must give glory to God in worship as he praises God; but even more because all conduct is worship, he must give glory to God in life and particularly in face of life's problems and disasters. This is a facet of theology expressed most clearly in the wisdom writings.

A modern writer has spoken of 'puzzled and frustrated men and women of this modern age to whom the Bible speaks in language no longer intelligible about things no longer credible'. The writers of *Proverbs* and the later book of Ecclesiasticus used well-known proverbial language to speak of common human experience. The introduction to Proverbs (1-9) is mainly devoted to an exhortation to respond to the call of

Wisdom, portrayed (because the word for wisdom is feminine in Hebrew) as a good and beautiful woman, attractive and friendly, interested in everyone and able to save men from the seductive allurements of an attractive but adulterous female called Folly'. The good life, or perhaps the better life, because it is usually painted in contrasts, to which Wisdom invites men, is a life that to the wise men is eschewing evil and reverencing God. This fact is made clear by the close link envisaged between God and Wisdom. Wisdom is God's gift, appropriated by complete reliance on God rather than on human insight or wisdom, and by diligent search. As the 'word' of God became almost a separate person revealing God, so 'wisdom' issuing in the good life reveals what God is. Wisdom was God's first creation, and became either his foreman builder or the child in whom he delighted (8.30); response to her, pictured as eating her bread and drinking her wine, will give men life (9.5).

The book of *Ecclesiastes* in sceptical terms attempted to break the earth-bound materialistic view of rewards and punishments that the prophetic teaching and the Deuteronomic writers had helped to fasten on to religion. All the aims for which men live—wealth, wisdom, posterity or religion—must be tested by the simple, inevitable fact of death. Wise men advised the enjoyment of food, work and wedlock as God's gifts to men; for their part men should be generous, honest and active in all the work God gives them to do, and while they should never let ignorance of the future prevent planning, they should ride loose to all material possessions. Although he had not reached it, the writer prepared the way for an attitude to life that regarded the rewards of religion as 'treasure in heaven', spiritual riches; he had seen the reaction of the rich fool when told 'tonight you will die; and then what will happen to all your possessions?'

The wonderfully dramatic book of *Job* carried this attitude to life much further. The writer had been driven deeper in an attempt to face the experiences of calamity, loss of loved ones, and acute physical suffering, perhaps the greatest test of belief in God.

In the prologue, God's pride in Job's goodness is represented as the cause of all his suffering, which was allowed in order to prove that the truly religious man will worship God though he lose everything by his devotion. The story is comparable to the psalm at the end of the book of Habakkuk:

> *Though the fig tree do not blossom,*
> *nor fruit be in the vines,*
> *the produce of the olives fail*
> *and fields yield no food,*
> *the flock be cut off from the fold,*
> *and there be no herd in the stalls;*
> *Yet I will rejoice in the Lord,*
> *I will joy in the God who delivers me.*

Or we may recall the reply of the Jewish youths when threatened with the fiery furnace: 'Our God whom we serve is able to deliver us; but if not, we will not serve your gods' (Dan. 3.17). It has been regarded as revealing a meaning of the cry of desolation on Calvary, when Jesus, stripped of his most precious possession, his fellowship with God, went on to give his life in complete trust.

In the three cycles of Job's dialogues with his three friends, the orthodox answers to the problem of evil and suffering are met and rejected: that suffering is the inevitable outcome of sin; that it is God's chastisement saving man by showing him the meaning of sin; that it is God's purging of man. Ezekiel's ingenious suggestion that wicked men are museum pieces preserved by God to justify his punishments is ignored (12.16). Job is gradually led, especially through the intervention of a fourth friend, Elihu, to turn from himself and seek God, from the self-centredness, self-pity and self-righteousness caused by the demand from his friends for self-examination, to a longing for a vision of God himself so that all the suffering and evil can be seen as part of God's will and purpose. Suddenly out of the storm God speaks, takes Job out into 'the picture gallery of his world' and shows him his wisdom, greatness and glory. In self-abasement Job replies:

I have heard of thee by the hearing of the ear,
but now my eye sees thee,
Therefore I despise myself and repent in dust and ashes. (42.5)

His repentance is not for the sins of which his friends had accused him but for that lack of humility, of reverence for the Lord, of living life in the light of the glory of God, which was the meaning of true religion to the wise men. Jesus himself said that suffering was not caused by the sins of a man or his parents, but that God should be glorified (John 9.3).

Man's Dependence on God

From a vision of the glory and majesty of God, comparable to that seen by Job, sprang the characteristic Old Testament belief that man is utterly dependent on God: 'he is your life and the length of your days' (Deut. 30.20). As today we ask, 'What is man? What is the purpose of his life? What is his destiny; does he end at the grave or is there some life beyond?' so in the Old Testament all these questions were answered in relation to God. Apart from God man has no beginning, meaning, purpose or end.

We have seen that in Hebrew thought man was pictured as a lump of clay, shaped by the divine potter and animated by the divine spirit or breath blown into his nostrils (Gen. 2). A similar picture, although with more knowledge of anatomy, is seen in Ezekiel's vision of the re-creation of Israel in the valley of dry bones (37). At the prophetic word heaps of bones, so dry that the marrow had gone from them, rattled together to form skeletons, they were flexed with sinews, packed round with flesh, and skin stretched over them. Then the wind, the breath or spirit of God, blew down the valley and made the dead forms stand on their feet, an exceeding great army. There was no thought of an immortal soul imprisoned in a mortal body, nor of a trichotomy of body, mind and spirit, or of thought, feeling and will. Body and divine breath made the whole man, who was a unity, completely dependent on God from whom he received his dignity. A psalmist wrote,

> *What is man that thou art mindful of him,*
> *And the son of man that thou dost care for him?*
> *Yet thou hast made him little less than God,*
> *And dost crown him with glory and honour.*
> *Thou hast given him dominion over the works of thy hands;*
> *Thou hast put all things under his feet.* (Ps. 8)

Without the spirit of God man had no life, but the spirit could invade man's personality with an intensity which gave him extraordinary power, physical strength (Judg. 14, 6), technical skill (Ex. 31), civil (Gen. 31) or military leadership (Josh. 1). God's spirit changed men's hearts (Ezek. 11), and supremely it made a man a preacher or prophet (Isa. 61). It came from God and was always under his control (Ps. 51.11).

> *These all look to thee,*
> *   to give them their food in due season.*
> *When thou givest to them, they gather it up;*
> *When thou openest thy hand, they are filled with good things.*
> *When thou hidest thy face, they are dismayed;*
> *When thou takest away their breath, they die and return to*
> *   their dust.*
> *When thou sendest forth thy Spirit, they are created;*
> *And thou renewest the face of the ground.* (Ps. 104)

Man's dependence on God is seen too in Old Testament ideas of the origin of man's righteousness. Hosea (10.12) told his hearers to sow righteous acts, and reap loving-kindness till the Lord comes and pours our righteousness like rain. Second-Isaiah further stressed God's initiative, 'the heavens pour down righteousness, the earth opens to receive it, and up-rightness and righteous acts sprout forth' (45.8); 'only in God is the righteous act and strength' (45.24).

From these concepts of man's dependence on God and the possibility of his fellowship with God arose some of the most important pictures of the meanings of sin, and the belief that death was not 'the last line of all'.

We have seen that to the writer of Genesis 3 sin that broke fellowship with God was deliberate disobedience to God's revealed will, grasping at equality with him and rejecting his lordship; but sin might be committed unknowingly, and so from our modern standpoint might not be a guilty act. When Jonathan put his stick in the wild honey and sucked it he had broken his father's vow to God, of which he had not heard (I Sam. 14), but he had sinned, the oracle was silent and God no longer spoke or guided. In one section of the Law (Num. 15) only such unwitting sins can be forgiven. Sin could also be the breach of custom or convention, 'not the done thing' (Gen. 20.9; 29.26). Often, especially in sex crimes, it is said that 'such a thing ought not to be done in Israel', and the act is called 'folly' or 'godlessness' (Gen. 34.7; II Sam. 13); customs or morals were not simply human but represented standards by which God judged.

An interesting picture is found in the word frequently translated 'sin'. It is the same word as is used to describe the seven hundred chosen, left-handed men of Benjamin who could sling stones at a human hair and not miss (Judg. 20.16). Sin is missing the target in life. By the end of the Old Testament period the target had become as high as the character of God, 'You shall be holy as I am holy' (Lev. 11.45); in the New Testament it is God-like perfection (Matt. 5.48), or 'the measure of the stature of the fullness of Christ' (Eph. 4.13). Another group of words for sin expresses the idea of something twisted or tortuous, and contains the metaphor of deviating or wandering off the straight, main road, perhaps into the Bypath Meadow that Bunyan pictured.

Each of these words portrays sin as a human act or attitude in relation to God. Even after adultery with Bathsheba and causing the murder of Uriah, David is represented as saying,

> *Against thee, thee only, have I failed,*
> *And done that which is evil in thy sight.* (Ps. 51)

But the word that espresses this wrong attitude to God most strongly is usually translated 'transgression'; it means 'rebellion', a deliberate organised revolt against a recognised authority whether parent or lord. The wicked man adds rebellion to missing the mark (Job 34.37), rejects the authority of God and turns from his glory.

The words used to express the experience of forgiveness and the restoration of a right relationship with God also emphasise the meaning of sin; some of them are brought together in the unsurpassed prayer for forgiveness in Psalm 51,

> *Be gracious to me, O God, according to thy covenanted love;*
> *According to the abundance of thy tender compassion rub out,*
>   *blot out the record of my rebellion;*
> *Wash me thoroughly (pounding or treading like a laundry*
>   *woman) from the stain that comes from getting off the road;*
> *Purify me, make me clean as the leper is pronounced clean*
>   *from his disease, and as the temple ritual removes the barriers*
>   *between God and man;*
> *For my rebellion I myself recognise now, my failure stares*
>   *me in the face continually.*

A post-biblical Jewish writer claimed that all things are pre-ordained by God and man has freewill. The same power to hold together two apparently incompatible opposites is seen in the theology of the Old Testament. Man has great dignity, crowned with glory and honour by God, and yet he is utterly dependent on God for life and righteousness, and in fellowship with God lies his only hope of immortality. All the initiative springs from God, but man must 'turn' and repent; he must trust, and wait hopefully upon God.

Life after Death

From belief in man's dependence on God grew the certainty that life does not end at the grave but is continued in fellowship with the same God whom men know here. Popular beliefs are seen in the story of the medium at Endor who brought up from Sheol the spirit of Samuel at Saul's request (I Sam. 28). Samuel was recognised by his cloak, called a god, and had the same power of prophecy as before death. The way spirits of the dead spoke was a familiar illustration for a prophet to use (Isa. 29.4). Abigail believed that the life of David could be bound up in the

bundle of the living with God (I Sam. 25.29). Stories were told
suggesting a belief that God could 'take' men to live with
himself without their passing through death. Elijah was taken
in a fiery chariot (II Kings 2.11), and Enoch walked with God
before God took him (Gen. 5.24). Prophets and Psalmists both
use phrases that speak of men as being taken up to heaven or
going down to Sheol, without the thought of a moral distinction corresponding to our ideas of heaven or hell. In neither
can man escape from God (Ps. 139; Amos 9.2); but in death
there is no remembrance of God and in Sheol none can give
him praise (Ps. 6.5).

Some Psalmists spoke of human bodies returning to the dust
from which God had created them and breath returning to the
God who first breathed it into man's nostrils (90; 104); and the
writer of Ecclesiastes doubted the truth of the newly formulated Greek doctrine of the immortality of the soul (3.19; 9.1).

But there are Psalms that contain a clear assurance that
even death cannot break the fellowship which, in this life, men
can experience with God.

> *Thou wilt not leave my soul in Sheol*
> *Nor let thy saint see corruption.*
> *Thou wilt make me know the path of life,*
> *Fullest joys are in thy presence,*
> *Pleasant things are in thy right hand for ever.* (16.10f.)
>
> *Surely God will redeem my soul from the power of Sheol,*
> *For he will take me.* (49.15)
>
> *As for me, I am continually with thee,*
> *Thou dost hold my right hand.*
> *With thy counsel thou dost guide me*
> *And afterwards with glory thou wilt take me.* (73.23f.)

As love was stronger than death so was fellowship with God;
and though death was the bourne from which no traveller
returned to give absolute proof of a life beyond—David said
of his dead child, 'I shall go to him, but he will not return to
me' (II Sam. 12.23)—yet the strength of fellowship with God
enabled men to enter death with the cry, 'Father, into thy hands

I commend my spirit.' Even in the Old Testament we can trace the beginning of a belief that the quality of life, the way a man lived, was more important than length of life. Early writers regarded length of days as the sign of God's favour, and to be gathered to the family grave full of years as the most honourable end; but saints, who were certain of their fellowship with God, learnt that to be continually in his presence was more highly to be prized.

Jesus, as reported in the fourth Gospel and the Epistles of John, swept away completely the importance of death. The great crisis in life is not death but conversion, which enables us here and now to enter eternal life. If we know God we have fellowship with him and we have passed from death to life; the transition is clear because 'We know that we have passed out of death into life, because we love the brethren, (I John 3.14). Death is sleeping or passing from one room to another in the father's house (John 14). Paul drew a picture from the cornfield where from the old grain springs life clothed in a new and beautiful form, whose shape could never have been imagined from the old dry seed (I Cor. 15).

Man's Oneness with God

In the Old Testament there are verses that seem almost to assert the oneness of God and man, as though the separation of 'I' from 'Thou', subject from object, had gone. Many of these verses are found in the hymns from the temple worship. Often God is called man's refuge or fortress (16.1; 27.1), and even more intimately, the house in which man dwells (90.1; 91.1f.). Amos had said that God was inescapable; if we try to flee from him by climbing into heaven or sinking to the underworld we shall meet him there (9.2); but the Psalmist goes further. God's intimate knowledge of man's life means that his thoughts are read by God, his words are heard before they have reached man's lips. If, fleeing from God, man flies with the speed with which the light of dawn spreads across the sky to the uttermost edge of the world's bounds, he discovers in surprise that it is God's hand that has been ahead of him guiding him and God's powerful right hand has borne him along. If he tries to hide himself in darkness, darkness itself shines with all the brightness of day because God is there. The God who is everywhere is also the God who is all-powerful. One picture after another is heaped up to express God's place in human life. He knits the embryo together, bones, sinews and muscles as it grows in the mother's womb. His eye sees the undeveloped embryo and weaves the veins as a woman embroiders a cloth with variegated threads. The whole story of man's life is written in God's book before it begins. The Psalmist sums it all up:

How precious to me are thy thoughts, O God!
How vast is the sum of them!
If I would count them they are more than the sand. (139.17)

Religion has been defined as thinking God's thoughts after him. The writer of this Psalm seems to be suggesting that really religion is letting the precious unnumbered thoughts and purposes of God pour or teem through man's mind into God's world. The connection of ideas suggests that the Psalmist is saying that man's being and life and all creation are thoughts of God. It is not that God is a thought in man's mind, but man is a thought in the mind of God.

The heavens declare the glory of God without sound or speech, and for us no language is adequate, however pregnant the words may have become with meaning from the experiences of countless generations.

EPILOGUE

THE THEOLOGY of the Old Testament flows out into the faith of two religions that have greatly influenced western civilisation, Judaism and Christianity. Judaism claims to be in the continuing tradition of the same nation whom, in the Old Testament, God chose and made his people; Christianity claims to be the spiritual outcome, the continuance of the powerful, forward movement of the purpose of God seen in the lines of the pattern traceable through the Old Testament. Both religions use the language and imagery of the Old Testament to express their faith, and the contents of its pages to illustrate and confirm their own beliefs about God and his saving acts; without it the meaning of these religions could not be understood nor the rich depth of their experiences of fellowship with the eternal God plumbed.

To both Judaism and Christianity the Old Testament contains a valid revelation of God, who spoke through its prophets and made his ways known through its history. But there is a sense in which both religions have distorted its theology for their own purposes. Judaism has tended to minimise, in its opposition to Christian interpretation, both the incompleteness and the hope which is a characteristic element in the Old Testament and which, as the writer of the Epistle to the Hebrews endeavours to show, was clearly recognised in the Old Testament itself. Christianity is in danger of giving to the book less value than did Jesus and the New Testament writers, and of treating its revelation as superseded and abrogated, rather than as fulfilled, and carried forward toward completion and perfection. The 'law' of the God of Sinai has been contrasted with the 'grace' of our Lord Jesus Christ, and many of the great words of the Old Testament have been falsely interpreted as having, primarily, a legal meaning rather than as being cradled in the community life of the People of God. As we have seen, in fact 'righteousness' and 'justification' are metaphors drawn not primarily from the law-courts but from the people's conscience; 'redemption' conveys a wealth of family duty, not legal obligations connected with slave-markets; and even the imagery of sacrifice and temple ritual speaks of barriers removed between man and God, of estrangement healed and a new 'at-one-ment' within the family of God.

The presentation of Old Testament theology has suffered from the fact that both Jewish and Christian writers regard their faith as God's final revelation, as though the mighty movement of God in the Old Testament has come to rest in them. Eichrodt wrote, 'Anyone who studies the historical development of the OT finds that throughout there is a powerful and purposive movement which forces itself on his attention. It is true that there are also times when the religion seems to become static, to harden into a rigid system; but every time this occurs the forward drive breaks through once more, reaching out to a higher form of life and making everything that has gone before seem inadequate and incomplete. This movement does not come to rest until the manifestation of Christ, in whom the noblest powers of the OT find their fulfilment. Negative evidence in support of this statement is afforded by the torso-like appearance of Judaism in separation from Christianity.'[1] But Christians should remember that the 'powerful and purposive movement' discernible in the Old Testament is evident also in the New which tells of the mightier works that will be done (John 14.12), of the Spirit that shall guide into all truth (16.13), of another Day of the Lord, and the time when all things shall be made new. There is a real sense in which the forward drive did not come to rest in the manifestation of Christ.

The study of Old Testament theology should enable us to trace the pattern of Divine activity on the walls of the past, hear God's voice through the prophets of Israel, and learn something

[1] Eichrodt, *Theology of the Old Testament*, vol. i, p. 26.

of the glory of God. We can see the same pattern running through the New Testament, hear the same voice in the Gospels, and see the same glory in the face of Jesus. The God of Abraham, Isaac and Jacob is the God of the living, and he is the living God whose activities can still be traced. His voice can be heard, and his glory seen, by us today.

FOR FURTHER READING

THE PURPOSE of this book will have been achieved if readers now turn to Walter Eichrodt's book *Theology of the Old Testament*, of which vol. 1 has been translated into English by J. A. Baker (SCM Press, London, and Westminster Press, Philadelphia, 1961) and to Gerhard von Rad's *Old Testament Theology*, vol. 1, translated by D. M. G. Stalker (Oliver and Boyd, Edinburgh, and Harper and Row, New York, 1962). Other recent shorter works on the subject in English are: Edmond Jacob, *Theology of the Old Testament*, translated by A. W. Heathcote and P. J. Allcock (Hodder and Stoughton, 1958); Th. C. Vriezen, *Outline of Old Testament Theology*, translated by S. Neuijen (Oxford, 1958); L. Köhler, *Old Testament Theology*, translated by A. S. Todd (Lutterworth Press, 1957); G. E. Wright, *God Who Acts* (SCM Press, 1952); N. W. Porteous, 'The Theology of the Old Testament' in *Peake's Commentary on the Bible*, revised ed. (Nelson, 1962).

These books show a great variety in arrangement of the Old Testament material, in the estimate of its historical accuracy, and in the permanent value given to its revelation of God particularly in relation to the New Testament.

Eichrodt's arrangement is, God and People, God and World, and God and Man. In the first volume the covenant relationship is regarded as basic, and the historical accuracy of the story of the covenant made through Moses is held to be essential to an understanding of Old Testament religion. In the other two volumes, still to be translated into English, the idea of the covenant drops into the background. *Von Rad* takes as his basis the traditions of Israel's history before the monarchy, contained in the great credal statements used in the cultus. He treats separately the theology of Genesis-Joshua, the prophets, and the remainder of the Old Testament. *Jacob* opens with a good account of the history of Old Testament theology and its relation to other studies, and then deals with aspects of God, actions of God, and the final triumph of God. *Vriezen* also arranges the material in themes; he has a long introduction and then discusses God, man, God and man, man and man, and God, man, and the world. *Köhler* has three main sections: God, Man, Judgment and Salvation. These all write from the Christian standpoint and discard some statements or ideas in the Old Testament as primitive, superseded or outside the main stream of Biblical religion.

The SCM Press publishes four scholarly books in which the relations of the two Testaments are discussed: *A Christian Theology of the Old Testament* by George A. F. Knight; *The Faith of Israel* by H. H. Rowley; *The Old Testament and Christian Faith*, essays edited by B. W. Anderson; *Essays on Old Testament Interpretation*, edited by Claus Westermann.

INDEX OF SCRIPTURE REFERENCES